Spanish Missions
of
TEXAS

SPANISH MISSIONS

of

TEXAS

BYRON BROWNE

THE
History
PRESS

Published by The History Press
Charleston, SC
www.historypress.net

Front cover: *Mission Concepcion Restored by Light* by Laura Hernandez.
Back cover, top left: Socorro Mission, El Paso; *top center*: St. Michael icon, Socorro Mission; *top right*: Convento of Mission San José; *bottom left*: Presidio San Elizario. *Image courtesy of author*; *bottom right*: façade of church at La Bahía Presidio. *Image courtesy of author.*

First published 2017

Manufactured in the United States

ISBN 9781467136303

Library of Congress Control Number: 2016950694

This book is dedicated to Giovanni di Pietro di Bernardone, whose singular vision has compelled millions to try and find new methods of bridging those insufferable chasms between us all.

CONTENTS

Acknowledgements

In no way does this book intend to shed any new light or bring into sharper focus new information about the Spanish colonial period in Texas. Most of that work was accomplished 100 to 150 years ago by historians and scholars with more resources. However, this writer is forever indebted to those who went in search of and translated the old Spanish records, journals, inventories and diaries. Without their previous work, much of this book would have been erroneous and, perhaps, dull. Scholars such as Casteñeda, Bolton, Weddle, Habig and Dunn, to name a few, are owed a debt by all of us for their tireless work. Also, those Franciscans and soldiers who maintained their journals and diaries, all while suffering the elements and attacks and being deprived of wants and needs—to these brave men I feel we are all indebted, perhaps in a way we do not yet realize. Men such as Bernal Díaz del Castillo and Fathers Espinosa and Morfi chronicled their times, somehow knowing that what they were engaged in was worthy of a place in history. To all of these men I am eternally grateful, as I believe all should be who take an interest in the past. Father Espinosa, the "Julius Caesar of the Spanish Colonial Period," surely was aware of the Ciceronian quote *Nescire autem quid ante quam natus sis acciderit, id est semper esse puerum* ("To not know what occurred before you were born is to be forever a child").

Many others have helped make the writing of this book possible, not the least my wife, Angie, who was more patient than I knew possible during all the late nights, very early mornings and missed appointments. To her I am forever obliged.

Similarly, as always, I am indebted to my son, Taylor, for his never-yielding encouragement and optimism.

Of the many others who offered their time and effort to this work, I am very grateful not only to have worked with them but simply to have shared their company for a few moments: Melissa Gonzales, formerly of the Witte Museum; Claudia Rivers, curator of the Special Archives Collection for the University of Texas at El Paso, and her excellent staff; Father David Garcia; Brother Ed Loch at the Diocese at San Antonio; Jared Ramirez with the Goliad State Park; Dr. Michael Strutt; Corey Snyder, a colleague with a kindred interest; Mrs. Marybeth Tomka, the head of collections at the Texas Archaeological Research Laboratory; Mr. Vincent Huízar, for his time and invaluable information; and the staff at the Dolph Briscoe Center for American History at the University of Texas at Austin.

There are, of course, many others who, in some way, contributed to this book's development, and I thank them all. If I have overlooked anyone obvious, please realize any oversight was an error of fatigue, not conscience.

INTRODUCTION

When faced with the complexity and magnitude of this subject, I confess that, in a way like Father Massanet, I was tempted to leave it as I had found it—unbounded, overgrown, wild and teeming with potential injury. The amount of work already completed on the Spanish missions in the United States is overwhelming. Dozens of missions and presidios stud the American landscape, from the Carolinas to California. Each has had dozens of writers and photographers pursuing their story for over two centuries. And each includes thousands of letters, invoices, requests, inventories and the ubiquitous complaints of the Franciscan missionaries, Spanish soldiers and regional politicians that fill hundreds of boxes at a few dozen institutions in the Southwest United States, Mexico and Spain. However, the subject is too intriguing to leave untried. Because the work was not yet completed, previous authors have not dealt with the restoration and reconstruction efforts that so many have labored over for so long. This book makes a small attempt to update the reader on the status of these Texas missions as they rest, today, in the twenty-first century.

The sixteenth century promised adventure and wealth for the Spanish crown. However, the errant journeys of Cabeza de Vaca, one of the four survivors of the Narváez expedition of 1527–28, procured a marvelously horrific narrative and yielded little in the way of riches for the Spanish government. Subsequent explorations by Vázquez de Coronado, de Soto, Espejo, Álvarez de Piñeda, Moscoso and even Oñate ended in much the same manner: defeat brought about through disease, exposure to the elements or lack of resources. The vaunted Seven Cities of Cibola, the fabled Seven Islands of Antille and Gran Quivira all were to exist and contain more gold and silver than the Spanish vault could maintain. For nearly a century, conquistadors and explorers ranged through an often fruitless and hostile territory that yielded very little as far as the crown was concerned. In 1629, however, a preternatural event turned the heads of the Spanish government and the hearts of its Franciscan missionaries.

Her name was María Coronel y de Arana. She was born in 1602 and raised in Agreda, a town in the north central portion of Spain. Agreda was known as a community where Christians, Arabs and Jews lived and worked together. At the age of sixteen, she took her orders; the family home, after a few years of wrangling from her father, was transformed into a convent. The entire immediate family devoted themselves to the principles and dictates of St. Francis. Akin to the brown, dun habits worn by the Franciscan brothers, the sisters of the Convent of the Immaculate Conception wore a white-and-blue habit. Once cloistered, María assumed the name Sister María de Jesús de Agreda. Beginning in 1620 and continuing for eleven years, Sister María is said to have had dreams of bilocation, wherein her spirit traveled to west Texas and eastern New Mexico to educate the natives in the ways of the Catholic faith. Indeed, in the summer of 1629, a delegation of the Jumano tribe walked to the Friary San Antonio de la Isleta in New Mexico to ask for more information regarding the lessons they had received. The *custos* (Latin for "guardian") of the friary, Father Alonso de Benavides, understandably perplexed, pressed the Indians for more information. They related how the "Lady in Blue" had given them instruction in the Christian faith for several years in their own language and was the personage who had directed them to the friary for further lessons and to ask for baptism. (Benavides mentions this episode in his extraordinary pamphlet *Memorial*, written in 1630 for Spain's King Philip IV.)

While a fascinating story that could be taken either to heart or *cum grano salis*, the revelation nevertheless had Father Benavides on a ship back to Spain to have a talk with the nuns at Saint Clare's. Sister María confessed that it was she who had had these adventures of bilocation. Even under the volatile scrutiny of the Inquisition, she swore that all of it was factual. The Franciscan Benavides knew immediately that here was proof of purpose. A Franciscan's goal was to spread the Word, and here was a clear directive.

Many historians and writers have included this saga in their own explanations for the Spanish endeavors into what would become Texas, because to omit the story would be tantamount to omitting the Moorish influence on Ferdinand and Isabella's decision to finance Columbus's voyages or its influence on the architecture of many of the missions. Agreda's story is included here for the same reason. While fanciful to some, its omission would deny an integral part of the story. Of course there are other, less fantastic reasons for the Spanish expansion efforts into the region, and the most singular reason is far more human than spiritual. In addition to the mines of what is today Coahuila, Mexico, there was silver, and a lot of it, in the mounds and mountains of New Mexico. Father Benavides knew that illustrating this fact for his sovereign would entice the crown to open the government's purse for more *entradas*—exploration efforts into the New World.

There was promise that the womb of the region just north of the Rio Grande teemed with the same wealth as the Aztecs had delivered to Hernán Cortés. Both the news of Columbus's discoveries in the late fifteenth century and the magnificent documenting of Cortés's missions through Mexico, as recorded by Bernal Díaz in the latter part of the sixteenth century, lured many adventurous Europeans to the Americas. And if the Spanish were coming, so, too, were the Franciscans. A papal bull from Alexander IV of May 3, 1493, mandated that Catholic emissaries be sent to the Americas—"worthy, God-fearing, learned, skilled and experienced men in order to instruct the inhabitants in the Catholic faith." Indeed, Bernal Díaz writes many times of the Franciscan brothers' attempts to dissuade the Indian priests from centuries of what they considered horrific, pagan religious practices. They proffered, in its stead, a religion that could allow for communal trust, amicability and, at the very least, the freeing of those people whom the Spaniards discovered in almost every village: caged, violently abused and waiting their turn to have their hearts torn from their chests. The Franciscans' restraint in not punishing the blood- and feces-encrusted priests was matched only by their devotion to convert and save. (Diaz tells us that Cortés, if the *Relijiosos'* efforts failed, used his own brand of conversion with the natives, usually with the business end of his *arquebus* [heavy gun].) They imagined that if they could maintain true to their vows in the face of such barbarity, they could certainly continue conversions with whomever waited beyond the borders of El Río del Norte. However, some tribes north of the Rio Grande were dissimilar from their southern cousins. While the tribes of central Mexico were certainly barbaric to a European's thinking, they also, in many instances, demonstrated some semblance of civilization: farms were maintained, animals were herded and buildings had a sense of permanency and purpose. Further, de León and Father Massanet remark that the tribes of east Texas were friendly and welcoming of the Spaniards' *entradas*. Nevertheless, many groups farther west were seminomadic, wandering from one cache to the next for seemingly wistful reasons. They raised no crops, because to do so would mean staying put for a while. They ate whatever they found while meandering across a near anemic land. To the Spanish mind, for many of these tribes religion consisted of little more than bemusement with the sun and moon. Just as a shepherd needs a distinct area for his flock, the Franciscans needed their subjects congregated and stationary. Unfortunately, this program was totally at odds with the culture of several of the natives within the region that would become Texas.

The systematic method employed by the Spanish in trying to colonize the northern Mexico and Texas region is unique and laudable. That the Spanish crown would consider and agree to the Franciscans' plans for conversion of the natives allows intimate insight into the character of those ultimately responsible for the decisions involving expansion. Over the centuries many empires have allowed exodus from and expansion for their countries. The ancient Greeks actively sought to subdue their own in Sicily and Magna Graecia (southern Italy); the British, many centuries later, simply could not leave their own to themselves; even the French government during this same colonial period, although employing Franciscan missionaries during their explorations, seems to have made little use of their talents as concerned the local populace. Conversely, the Spanish encouraged their citizens (many of them Canary Islanders) to relocate to both Nueva España and the Nuevas Filipinas, as Texas was, at times, called. The Franciscans who accompanied and oftentimes led these excursions into Texas were as determined in purpose as their progenitor, St. Francis, had been. These Spanish religious viewed the territories north of Mexico as fecund land but a terrain where thousands of *gentiles* roamed spiritually inanimate. The Franciscans were determined to make converts of the natives, as their order mandated.

It would be naive to think that political motives were not also in play. Primarily, the crown knew that a native populace converted to Catholicism could become citizens de jure, and there is ample evidence that not only Spanish soldiers, immigrants and politicians but even, at times, the religious helped themselves to whatever produce—material or muscle—the natives could offer once they were secured within mission walls. Indeed, two events within only five years of each other in the late seventeenth century would motivate Franciscan missionaries into *la tierra adentro*, the territory north of the Rio Grande. The first, the Pueblo Revolt of 1680, scattered the Spanish colonies congregated in New Mexico eastward to present-day

El Paso. The second event, which appears to have troubled the Spanish government in Madrid the most, was the trespass of La Salle on the Texas coast in 1685. These two occurrences, coupled with the visions of the "Lady in Blue," enflamed the Franciscans' ardent desire to carry out their work. Nevertheless, as we will see, the Franciscans were more concerned with the arc of history, with the frighteningly beautiful trajectory of the work of saving souls than the pressing, controlling minutiae of the military and politicians.

This book is dual in purpose, as were the Spanish government's expeditions into the New World. In Texas (including Louisiana in the same region) as in New Mexico, Arizona and California, the missionaries' ventures were singularly aimed toward the heavens, while those of the officials, immigrants and soldiers were more base. This work is an effort both to recall that history and its impact and to allow the reader an opportunity to witness just what has become of all that time and expended energy. The stories of the Spanish missions reveal the totality of the paths of the mind and will; these stories illustrate duplicity and duality and are simultaneously shameful and shameless, dim and profound, sacrilegious and sacred. In short, they represent all that is human.

CHAPTER 1

EARLY ENTRADAS AND HISTORY

The Franciscans' efforts in Texas can ultimately be thought of as taking their beginnings from those Spanish conquistadors who went in search of riches and resources to finance their system of *encomienda*: a demi-feudal system whereby the Spanish were allowed, under Spanish law, to offer indigenous populations protection from hostilities and instruction in the Catholic faith in exchange for tribute and possession of whatever land they could wrangle. Of course, this more often meant the enslavement of the natives, forced labor and physical abuses. This system was so abused by the *encomenderos* that it was terminated by the Castilian government in 1730. Nevertheless, it was the lure of potential and enduring wealth that drove young Europeans to the New World by the thousands. And any groups that tried to venture across the Atlantic were sure to be accompanied by religious faculty as well.

The oldest missions in Texas were established in the El Paso region. But Álvarez Pineda, who is said to have been the first European to view and map the Texas coastline, in 1519, can be ultimately credited as the catalyst for the Texas missions' establishments. His expedition, financed by Francisco de Garay, then governor of Jamaica, called for Pineda to sail from Jamaica and begin his cartography of the coast from where de León had left off at Florida. Just as for de León and Velásquez before him, Pineda's ultimate goal was to find a new passage to the Pacific Ocean—the Strait of Anian. Pineda was to sail west from Florida; indeed, his mapping of the Gulf of Mexico is the earliest littoral evidence of the region. Pineda's efforts were famously scotched when Cortés felt trespassed upon by Pineda's scouts as they attempted to reconnoiter Villa Rica de la Vera Cruz, today's Vera Cruz, Mexico. (Pineda's small fleet left the harbor a mere six weeks after Cortés had left Cuba for his own excursion into Mexico.) Ever true to his character, Cortés arrested these men, confronted the younger Pineda and caused their regress back up the Mexican coastline to Río Pánuco near present-day Tampico. There Pineda attempted to install a Spanish settlement.

While very little is known of Pineda's settlement, he is credited with being the first to show that Florida is not an island, as De León had surmised, but, rather, peninsular. Additionally, Pineda has the distinction of being the first European to locate the great delta of the Mississippi River. Although many writers contest this, claiming instead that Pineda found another river's mouth in Alabama or one farther east, the evidence from the *cédula*, or official report, left for Garay is difficult to dispute. Pineda named the site Río del Espíritu Santo ("River of the Holy Spirit"), since this opening was sighted either on or very close to the Catholic feast day of Pentecost, Espíritu Santo.

What is known of Pineda after his encampment on the Río Pánuco is a sad matter to relate. After Pineda was driven northward up the Mexican coast by Cortés, his colony was found by Diego de Camargo, the captain of a ship of supplies for Pineda's settlement. Pineda's unfortunate end is recounted, somewhat disinterestedly, by Bernal Díaz del Castillo, one of Cortés's officers:

> *While we were lying at Villa Segura, Cortés was informed by letter that one of the vessels which Garay had fitted out for the object of forming settlements on the river Pánuco had arrived at Vera Cruz. This vessel was commanded by a certain Comargo, and had on board above sixty soldiers, but who were all in very bad health, with their stomachs largely swelled. This Comargo related how unfortunately Garay's expedition to the river Pánuco had terminated. The Indians had massacred the commander-in-chief Álvarez Pineda, with the whole of his troops and horses, and then set fire to his vessels. Comargo alone had been fortunate enough to escape with his men on board one of the vessels, and had steered for Vera Cruz, where they arrived half famished, for they had not been able to procure any provisions from the enemy. This Comargo, it was said, had taken the vows of the order of the Dominicans. Comargo and his men, by degrees, all arrived at Villa Segura; which indeed took a considerable time, for they were so weakened that they could scarcely move along. When Cortés saw in what a terrible condition they were, he recommended them to our care, and*

showed Comargo and all his men every possible kindness. If I remember rightly, Comargo died soon after, and also several of his men. We used to call them, jokingly, verdigris bellies, from the immense size to which the latter were swollen, and the death-like appearance of the men.[1]

From the information we have today, it seems the Huastec Indians (among whom Pineda had settled) revolted as soon as the supply ship arrived. It would also appear that the natives waited until the supplies were offloaded, since Camargo and his men arrived emaciated and dying of their wounds. A bitter irony is the fact that those men who had survived their time with Pineda, at first repulsed by Cortés and then escaping from Pánuco, were conscripted into Cortés's army for his assault on the Mexican capital of Tenochtitlán, presumably during the later siege campaign of 1521. Nevertheless, it was Pineda's expedition, in conjunction with Cortés's, that advanced Spanish interests.

Only six years later, the ill-fated Narváez expedition departed from Santo Domingo with the goal of colonizing the region between Florida and today's Tampico, Mexico. Narváez had received license to install settlements in the gulf region from Carlos I. However, it is difficult to understand why the king would entrust such an enterprise to Narváez. The latter had been sent, in 1520, to intercept and arrest Cortés in Mexico. It was Narváez who was taken captive by Cortés and imprisoned for two years before being dismissed to Spain, many of his troops conscripted by Cortés. Nevertheless, the expedition of Narváez was as doomed as that of Pineda. Over 140 of his soldiers deserted while anchored at Hispaniola, followed by the loss, in a hurricane, of at least two of his six ships while en route to what he reasoned was the east coast of Mexico. Narváez landed instead on the west coast of Florida in April 1528. The Spanish king did, however, exhibit sound judgment in one aspect of this expedition: he employed Álvar Núñez Cabeza de Vaca as both second in command and treasurer for the king's "Royal Fifth" when and if any riches were found. Of Narváez's leadership skills and prowess as conquistador, we can only say that all of it was lost somewhere in the chaos of the Gulf of Mexico. Of the nearly 1,000 men who left Spain with Narváez, only 4 ever returned. We can be grateful that Cabeza de Vaca was in that tiny group.

The stories and adventures of Cabeza de Vaca are multiple and varied. Shipwrecked and alone in a desolate, hostile environment, Cabeza de Vaca not only survived but, in a fashion, flourished during his eight years wandering southwest Texas and the interior of Mexico. At one time imprisoned by the natives, then empowered as a merchant-trader and later idolized as a healer, Cabeza de Vaca turned his experiences into one of the most incredible tales ever recounted. Similar to the tragic and mystifying wanderings of Odysseus, Cabeza de Vaca did not find his way back to a Spanish settlement until 1536, having wandered a little over eight years and approximately 2,400 miles by foot before reaching his Ithaca, the Spanish colony of San Miguel de Culiacan. His book, entitled *Comentarios*, then *La relación*, was subsequently retitled *Naufragios* ("The Shipwrecked"). Cabeza de Vaca wrote not only of his experiences but also of the many Indian tribes he encountered. His is the first book published on the subject of the New World. As harsh as much of Cabeza de Vaca's tale was, it still held enough spark to kindle more Spanish exploration in the region.

In 1540, Francisco Vásquez de Coronado y Luján made his famous entrada north of the Rio Grande in search of the gold-saturated Seven Cities of Cibola. This enterprise had Coronado reaching from New Mexico to Kansas. In 1539, as governor of Nueva Galicia (present-day Mexican states of Jalisco and Sinaloa), Coronado assembled a preliminary entrada into New Mexico with the clear purpose of determining whether the territory might contain wealth of a magnitude similar to that which Cortés had taken. This mission was led by Fray Marcos de Niza and Estevanico, the Moorish slave who was another of the four survivors of the Narváez expedition. This group entered today's southeastern Arizona and then headed east. An impatient Estevanico hurried ahead of the expedition to find the Zuni pueblo he and Cabeza de Vaca had heard mentioned just a few years prior. When Father de Niza arrived at the Zuni settlement, he found Estevanico dead of multiple arrow wounds. The friar's report to Coronado, *Descubrimiento de las siete Ciudades*, suggests that Estevanico's lewd behavior with the native women of Cibola (a Zuni pueblo) was the cause. Evidently fearful that he could suffer the same fate as Estevanico, Fray de Niza returned to Coronado, having seen Cibola only from a distance. However, his visions of the many pueblos seem to have convinced Coronado that the tales suggested by both Cabeza de Vaca and de Niza were factual. One year later, Coronado assembled a large contingent of a few hundred European soldiers, along with approximately 1,400 Mexican Indian auxiliaries, and began his own expedition into the territory.

The initial entrada by Coronado led him into eastern Arizona, where he and his men (a small contingent had been sent by sea with provisions) came upon the settlement of Hawikuh. The expedition promptly overran the village when entry was not offered. Having sent an expeditionary party westward (it was this segment of Coronado's men that discovered the Grand Canyon and Colorado River), Coronado was enticed by an Indian named *Bigotes* ("the mustached one") to trek westward to the Tiguex region, a series of pueblos in southeastern New Mexico established along the Rio Grande. It was here in the winter of 1540–41 that Coronado again chose to take by force what could possibly have been gifted had a less bellicose attitude prevailed.

Coronado decided to establish his winter quarters in a pueblo that the Spaniards called Coofor. The one dilemma facing the Spanish was that this pueblo was already occupied. Rather than offering any sort of compromise, Coronado ordered the exodus of the natives from their own homes in the middle of winter. Augmenting the injury, the Spaniards kept all the resources the pueblo contained. When the Tiwas Indians resisted by killing several of the Spanish horses and other livestock, Coronado commanded a "fire and blood" campaign that resulted in the deaths of hundreds of the native residents. The Tiguex War witnessed not only these hundreds of deaths but also the enslavement of dozens of women. This resulted in the abandonment of the neighboring pueblos; the natives were either killed or retreated to the mountains. Even a casual reading of the Tiguex War narrative illustrates the brutality of these early entradas. At this point, the Spanish interests were focused almost exclusively on wealth. Indeed, seemingly unmoved by the slaughter of the indigenous population, Coronado was lured farther east by another Indian. Given the moniker *El Turco* ("the Turk"), this Pawnee native broadcast that there was, to the east, a civilization called Quivira that bristled with both riches and a populace of potential mine laborers. Coronado, easily convinced, meandered through the Texas panhandle and finally reached the fabled Quivira (in today's Kansas, although this area, too, has been contested through the past century) in 1541. He discovered only grass-thatched huts and endless herds of buffalo along the way. Suspected and interrogated, the Turk confessed to purposefully leading Coronado's men away from the Zuni territory solely so that the region could be free of Spanish domination. Before the expedition returned to New Mexico, the Turk was garroted. A frustrated Coronado, after one more winter in New Mexico during which his group was constantly harassed by the Tiwas Indians in hit-and-run raids, returned to Nueva Galicia in April 1542. Reports of his brutalities, having reached Mexico City and then Madrid, resulted in his own interrogation, although his punishment was far less severe than those he inflicted.

Coronado's expedition can only be described as a failure when one considers what his intent had been. Clearly blinded by a future layered in gold, his mistake was entrusting himself to those on whom he was making war. The Indians would use this tactic several more times during the next century and a half. In fact, a little over a century later, Bernardo de Miranda was duped into pursuing what he was told were huge silver deposits in the Llano River area by Apache Indians, a tale "to parallel the stories of the cities of gold told to the gullible Coronado in an effort to lure his troops onto the Great Plains, where the Indians believed they would perish."[2] Modern history, however, construes his story as a courageous entry into the New World, an adventure like the first space explorations—although bare of tangible treasure, nevertheless cutting a path whereby others might follow. Conversely, two Franciscan friars chose to remain with the Zuni after Coronado retreated to Nueva España. Not long after, they were martyred for their efforts. After the brutality of Coronado, it is not difficult to imagine the Indians' suspicions. Accordingly, there were few Spanish excursions into this region for nearly forty years. After the egress of Coronado, the Zuni pueblos were re-inhabited, only to be vacated again thirty-nine years later when the next Spanish explorers advanced into the territory.

In the fifteenth and sixteenth centuries, Spain had, in a sense, near complete domination of the areas from the Caribbean to California. With the exception of entradas by Antonio de Espejo (in the southwest of Texas) and Luis de Moscoso Alvarado (in the northeast), there were several, though minor, expeditions into a region that was infamous for both its scarcity of resources and hostile native population. Still, in the years between Coronado and Alonso de León with Fray Damián Massanet (sometimes "Mazanet"), an approximate 140 years, the Spanish government continued to cross the Rio Grande in order to gather slave labor from the native tribes for the silver mines in the Mexican state of Coahuila. Somewhat apart from this sort of enterprise, the Spanish also delegated other entradas deeper into the heart of Texas with the aim of locating, for the crown, more wealth and, for the Franciscans, more souls for conversion.

In 1650, Hernan Martín and Diego del Castillo left from Santa Fe under orders to explore north central Texas. During their expedition, they came upon a confederation of Indian tribes that the Spanish referred to as the *Tejas*—most likely from the word these natives used by way of greeting. These tribes seemed more friendly, more civilized (their settlements included huts and cultivated lands) and, as far as the Franciscans were concerned, more agreeable to the idea of reverting from their pagan worship to the Catholic ideology. Four years later, spurred on by the pearls that del Castillo had brought back from the Nueces River (present-day Concho), another

SPANISH EXPANSION into TEXAS

Early Spanish exploration routes, seventeenth century. *Image available on the Internet and included in accordance with title 17 U.S.C. Section 107.*

expedition was directed at the same area. This entrada was led by Diego de Guadalajara. Following the same route as the others, Guadalajara also came upon a friendly tribe, the Jumanos, who warned the Spanish not to travel any farther west, since the tribes there were at war with one another. A smaller Spanish unit sent ahead to reconnoiter was attacked by the warring factions. Nevertheless, the Spaniards, true to form, killed many and took nearly two hundred prisoners. Guadalajara returned to New Mexico solely due to lack of martial supplies.

The hostilities the Spanish often encountered while settling the territories around the Mexican states of Nuevo Leon and Coahuila were not solely aimed at them. What they found were dozens of disparate tribes on both sides of the Rio Grande, constantly waging war on each other. Those Franciscans trying to mollify and convert, in their terms, *indios rebeldes* (unconverted and recalcitrant to the Catholic idea) into *indios reducidos* (those either willing to be converted or already having sought it out through missionaries) had the initial task of trying to declare truces among the tribes. A few Franciscan missionaries had some success in these regions, but their efforts were singular; that is, they traveled and stayed among the natives alone. However, the warring continued, both intertribal and against the Spanish if they interfered, and the silver mines of northern Mexico were often in the way. One attempt to quell the fighting was undertaken in 1655 by Fernandez de Azcue. He, along with approximately one hundred Spanish soldiers and a few hundred Indian auxiliaries, attacked and defeated a very pugnacious Cacaxtles tribe. While considered a successful expedition (especially as this expedition is said to be the first documented crossing of the lower Rio Grande by a European), it quickly became evident that more would need to be done in order to pacify the entire region. Even though it was twenty years coming, the Bosque-Larios expedition of 1675 had exactly this mission in mind.

Earlier, in 1670, Indians from the regions around Nuevo Leon, Nueva Vizcaya and Coahuila had dispatched delegates to Spanish towns asking for guidance and direction in the Catholic faith. The historian Herbert Bolton writes, "It is clear that for several years some of the Indians of Coahuila and even from beyond the Rio Grande had been asking for missionaries, and, under what influences we do not know, had sent messengers to Saltillo, Parral, Guadalajara and Mexico City to seek them."[3] It would appear that, given the time period and documentation, one could be influenced by the María de Agreda story. Also at this time, these Indian emissaries did have the good fortune to encounter Fray Juan Larios, who agreed to accompany the natives to the edge of the Coahuila region, alone, and stayed nearly three years among them. Robert Weddle states, "They were the Coahuiltecans, divided into a large number of small tribes and bands which dwelt on both sides of the Rio Grande. Like children lost in darkness the Coahuiltecans stood on the northern frontier of New Spain, beckoning to the missionary fathers to come and show them the light."[4] By the end of 1674, Father Larios had completed three *converso* missions to the area, the latter two accompanied by a couple more religious. By 1675, the situation was such that the Spanish government felt secure enough to try to colonize the region.

In April 1675, Fernando del Bosque, a Spanish soldier appointed by Antonio Balcárcel, the *alcalde mayor*, or governor of Coahuila, led an entrada to the north that began from the existing Mission Nuestra Señora de Guadalupe in Coahuila. Among the group was a small contingent of Spanish soldiers again coupled with an auxiliary unit of Indian support and Frays Juan Larios and Antonio de San Buenaventura y Olivares. In May of the same year, this expedition reached the Rio Grande, most likely just below what is today Eagle Pass, Texas. Bosque officially claimed possession of the site and promptly named the river San Buenaventura del Norte. According to his report, once the expedition crossed the river, several Indian chiefs from various tribes approached the group, asking for religious instruction and baptism. Because baptism is a sacrament, instruction is required of the recipient as a prerequisite to its completion. The religious in the group promised the Indians that they would return for that purpose.

Bosque, in his formal report, recommended establishing missions in the area. Standard delays preceded the missions' establishment, but less than a decade later, political events would quash the discussions and speed these missions' development. The French, primarily in the form of explorer René Robert Cavelier, Sieur de la Salle, alarmed the Spanish government by their perceived trespass into the Gulf region.

The Spanish, and indeed many of the powers of western Europe, had, since the late fifteenth century, considered the southwest territory of the New World, whether settled or not, to be under Spanish dominance. That is, until the English—along with "God's Wind and Waves"—defeated the famous Spanish Armada in 1588. Although not as complete a rout as the opposition may have hoped, it does appear to have given promotion to the idea that pressing deeper into the New World, even those areas considered Spanish, was possible.

For decades the English, Dutch and French had settled territories in the Northeast, Canada and, to a lesser degree, some Caribbean areas. Nearly a century after the armada's defeat, La Salle traveled down the full scale of the Mississippi River, sliding on the iced-over upper quarter in the middle of winter and canoeing the rest of the way after the thaw. Along this trek he claimed everything contingent on both sides of the river for France; in the South, these territories included what would become Louisiana and a segment of Texas.

Interestingly, La Salle had, as a very young man, gained entrance to a Jesuit order. When the time came for full commitment, an act requiring rejecting his family's inheritance, he discovered a quite different employment. He sailed to Canada, where his older brother was already in residence as a priest in Montreal. He spent a few years foraging around and through the Great Lakes area before determining to find a southward passage to the Gulf of Mexico along the Mississippi. His intent was to establish trading posts all along the river system, a remarkably prescient idea from a business perspective.

Here should be mentioned a rather pernicious and disgraced Spaniard named Diego Dionisio de Peñalosa Briceño y Berdugo. Born in Peru, Peñalosa's life and character were so noxious as to make an ancient Roman dictator smirk. Due to his family's influence, he was made alcalde of Peru, but he became a fugitive from that country after corruption charges forced him from office. He escaped to Nueva España, where, by whatever circumstances, he was again placed in a position of authority as governor of New Mexico. During this term of office, the number of charges against him could not be ignored by the Inquisition. His deleterious behavior extended to arresting Alonso de Posada, then the Franciscan *custos* of the New Mexico missions, when the latter accused Peñalosa of misconduct, from illegally seizing property to abuses among the indigenous populace the Franciscans were trying to convert. A second time, in 1664, Peñalosa fled the charges rather than face them. At this time, seeking revenge, he approached the English in 1670 with the idea of establishing a settlement near the mouth of the Mississippi River so as to have a base for attacking Spanish interests in Nueva España as well as those areas north of the Rio Grande. Rejected by the English, Peñalosa retreated to France and again described the same scenario for King Louis XIV. This plan, too, was rejected. It is an interesting coincidence that Peñalosa's final attempt to persuade the French king took place one year before La Salle was assigned the task and that both men died the same year, 1687.

Having traversed the entirety of the Mississippi River from the frozen Illinois River to the mouth of the Mississippi in 1682, La Salle returned to France the next year to ask permission and funding for establishing a settlement at the end of the Mississippi at the Gulf of Mexico. Louis XIV agreed, and La Salle sailed from France in 1684 by royal decree to found a French settlement at the mouth of the Mississippi River. This final expedition of La Salle's was dramatically horrible, and one would be hard-pressed to count a single positive achievement from the enterprise. In fact, this venture, like those of the Donner Party or the Gallipoli campaign, is remarkable for its incredible failure. Losing a storage ship to pirates at Hispañola, angering the Karankawa Indians for borrowing too many of their canoes and finally ambushed and murdered by a few of his own, despairing men, La Salle's last voyage served only to anger the Spanish government for what it deemed encroachment on sovereign land. It did, however, have the effect of speeding the Spanish missions' efforts.

La Salle's expedition left Rochefort, France, in August 1684 with over three hundred sailors and settlers and almost immediately experienced trouble. Not yet clear of France, one of the four boats, the naval escort ship *Joly*, had to enter port for repairs. Once across the Atlantic, La Salle's expedition needed to find a port for resupplying before continuing on. However, enduring quarrels between La Salle and the commander of his four-vessel fleet, Tanguy le Gallois Beaujeu, resulted in the fleet losing much time in the Caribbean. Beaujeu made port at Petit Gouave rather than Port de Paix. Both ports are in present-day Haiti, but the former is much farther south and in the lower jaw of the great mouth of the Haitian bay, while the latter is situated on the northern coast and had been the rendezvous point for the fleet. Two of La Salle's other ships finally caught up with the *Joly* several days later; however, these delivered very disturbing news. As Henri Joutel, a soldier accompanying the expedition and one of the few to ever return to France, relates:

> *Two of our ships, which had been separated from us on the 18th of September, by the stormy Winds, arriv'd at Petit Gouave on the 2d of October. The Joy conceiv'd on Account of their Arrival, was much allay'd by the News they brought of the Loss of the Ketch, taken by two Spanish Piraguas; and that Loss was the more grievous, because that Vessel was laden with Provisions, Ammunitions, Utensils and proper Tools for the setting of our new Colonies; a Misfortune which would not have happen'd, had Monsieur de Beaujeu put into Port de Paix.*[5]

The loss of the ketch, fittingly named the *St. Francis*, would prove very helpful to the Spanish soon enough. But further misfortunes remained for La Salle. Several of the soldiers deserted once in the West Indies, and continued disputes with Beaujeu resulted in the group missing the mouth of the Mississippi, instead landing at Matagorda Bay off the Texas coast, nearly four hundred miles west of their objective. The other supply ship, the *Aimable*, was lost when it was run aground and, while stranded sideways, was cracked in two during an evening of hostile winds and violent waves. Although many supplies had been offloaded after its grounding, most were still aboard; no one suspected that such violence could occur to the vessels while the crews rested. Nonetheless, Joutel suspected Beaujeu:

> *The Ship was stranded on the Shoals. The ill management of the Captain, or of the Pilot, who had not steer'd by the Stakes placed for that Purpose… the sounding upon the Shoals to no Purpose, and several other Circumstances reported by the Ship's Crew and those who saw the Management, were infallible Tokens and Proofs, that the Mischief had been done designedly and advisably, which was one of the blackest and most detestable Actions that Man could be guilty of.*[6]

Soon afterward, in February 1685, La Salle, intent on maintaining his purpose, founded his settlement, which came to be referred to as Fort St. Louis, on Garcitas Creek (a stream running north out of Port Lavaca, southeast of Victoria, Texas). The encampment was constructed from locally cut trees and whatever detritus could be stripped from the *Aimable*. Many of his companions did not share his enthusiasm for the future and complained about returning home. Of the two ships remaining, the *Joly* and the *Belle* (the latter excavated in 1995 off the Texas coast), the former was loaded with provisions and the pessimistic and then set sail for France. Of those who remained, disease, despair and hostile Indians wore down both their numbers and resolve. La Salle knew only that he was lost in what must have appeared to be a wasteland. At first he tried to trek westward in an effort to find the Mississippi, the sole area with which he was familiar. Thereafter, better realizing his true location, he tried scouting to the east. It was during a second excursion eastward, with seventeen men, that a few members decided they had had enough. One Pierre Duhaut, in confederation with a few others, murdered six of La Salle's men while they slept and then later dispatched their commander. As Joutel relates, "The traitor Duhaut fired his Piece and shot Monsr. de la Sale thro' the Head, so that he dropp'd down dead on the Spot, without speaking one word."[7]

After this deed, six of the group continued north to Canada and eventually France, Joutel among them. A few others decided to remain among the Indians in east Texas, most likely the Hasanai, natives of the Tejas group. Those who had been left behind at Fort St. Louis, those too young or weak to try and make the journey east, were in a desperate situation. They waited two years for news of rescue, which never came. Most were never to learn the truth about La Salle's final venture. The Karankawa Indians, from whom La Salle had continually taken resources for his excursions and with whom he had had many arguments, decided, after they learned of La Salle's death and the departure of most of the more capable soldiers, to attack the settlement. During the 1688 attack, all of the inhabitants were massacred, save for five children, who were taken and incorporated into the tribe; four of them were the renowned Talon children.

It was this French excursion—this trespass, as the Spanish viewed it—that ultimately compelled the Spanish to proceed with their expansion efforts into *la terra adentro*, the land beyond.

Up to this point the story of the Franciscans' efforts to establish missions among the indigenous tribes of northern Nueva España had been told almost exclusively from the perspective of those in the West. The natives of New Mexico already had witnessed several Spanish entradas and settlements among their pueblos. However, news of La Salle's expedition soon reached the offices of the viceroys within the districts of New Spain. It was this singular event that redirected the Spanish focus to the east. In fact, even before La Salle's murder, the Spanish were mustering men to locate the intrusive French. After the seizure of the French ketch off of Santo Domingo in 1685, the French prisoners had an interesting tale to tell.

As to the number of search-and-destroy missions the Spanish convened for the purpose of locating La Salle, each historian and writer has a different answer. It is sufficient to say that at least three naval operations sailed from eastern Mexican to scout the Texas coast, and at a minimum, four land operations were organized for this purpose. During the land operations, between 1685 and 1689, a very experienced and capable soldier named Alonso de León (or *El Mozo*, "junior") led the four intra-territory expeditions to find and eradicate the French from Spanish lands. The first two yielded no results. The third expedition, in 1688, was undertaken after it was learned that a white man was living among the natives north of the Rio Grande. Crossing the Rio Grande, this time in a more northeast direction, the members of the expedition discovered that the report was true; a Frenchman named Jean Géry, an early deserter of the La Salle expedition, was living among the Coahuiltecan Indians and, moreover, had risen to a prominent position within their community. De León convinced the aged and confused Frenchman to return with him to Mexico, where Géry was interrogated. Even though Géry's answers to the viceroy's questions were rambling and oftentimes incoherent, he did offer a map to the location of Fort St. Louis and accompanied de León on his fourth venture across the Rio Grande. This journey would provide the truth and results that the Spanish had been hoping for.

Mention must be made of those who were to prepare the way for the missions that would soon appear in the Tejas lands of east Texas. In 1683, a delegation of twenty-four Franciscans (sources disagree on the number) sailed to New Spain for the purpose of founding a *colegio* or college, wherein these *relijiosos* could congregate, prepare and receive instruction before journeying into the volatile *gentilidad*, or pagan territories. When their small group, part of a larger supply mission, made port at Vera Cruz, their work began immediately. They found that a couple thousand pirates had just pillaged the port, killing or injuring the men and kidnapping the women. All the gold and silver that had been stacked and was waiting for retrieval to Spain had been taken. The friars literally stepped from the boat into the carnage of the dead, dying and wounded. These priests, only recently ordained and just arrived, "consoled and confessed the living, administered final rites, and gave proper burial to the dead."[8] This was their welcome to the realities of the New World, to which they had dedicated their lives.

Replica Mission San Francisco
in east Texas. *Image available on
the Internet and included in accordance
with title 17 U.S.C. Section 107.*

When they had done what was necessary, they were dismissed to Querétaro, walking in pairs to the northwest for nearly three hundred miles.

These friars established the missionary center of Colegio de la Santa Cruz de Querétaro. Among the college's first members, two are vital to the story of the Texas missions: Fathers Francisco Hidalgo and Damián Massanet. It was Hidalgo who, embarking northward from Querétaro, preached to the natives in the region of what is today northeastern Mexico. Making his way on foot, as his progenitor St. Francis had done, Hidalgo soon was followed by hundreds of devotees wherever he went. From all evidence, Hidalgo practiced what he preached and literally led by example, just as Francis had accumulated thousands of souls during his meanderings through Europe and the Middle East. Just over two hundred miles northwest of Querétaro, Hidalgo, accompanied by two other friars, arrived at Zacatecas, where his emotive teachings proved so effective that before the Franciscans were to leave, the town was clamoring that another missionary college be established there. The Franciscans replied that they were unable to comply, due to a lack of resources. However, in 1707 a second colegio, that of Nuestra Señora de Guadalupe de Zacatecas, was in fact founded. Such was the effect of these early friars' teachings that the numbers of those asking for conversion and instruction far exceeded the Franciscans' abilities to reach them. But Hidalgo was not the only ardent religious member to proceed with vehemence and purpose. Fray Massanet was to prove just as fervent in his quest.

The count of Monclova, Mexico, selected Alonso de León (who had also been appointed governor of Coahuila in 1687) as general to head up the entrada to locate the colony of La Salle. This expedition was to include not only fifty soldiers from the presidios within the province of Nueva

Vizcaya but another fifty from the provinces of Coahuila and Nuevo León. Accompanying these, besides the usual ancillary mule drivers and slaves and the still semi-bewildered Géry, were two religious personnel, Fray Toribio Garcia de Sierra, vicar of the province of Coahuila, and the very determined Father Damián Massanet. Speaking to the need and shortage of religious for such expeditions, Massanet was given his orders to accompany the de León entrada while trying to maintain Mission San Bernardino de la Caldera, a mission he had founded only a short time before in the northern Mexican interior. Even so, Massanet was a very eager companion, as he wrote in a letter to his friend Don Carlos de Sigüenza y Góngora:

> *At this time I was living at the Mission Caldera, in the province of Coahuila, whither I had gone with the intention of seeing whether I could make investigations and obtain information about the interior of the country to the north and northeast, on account of facts gathered from a letter now in my possession, which had been given in Madrid to our Father Fray Antonio Linaz. This letter treats of what the blessed Mother María de Jesus de Agreda made known in her convent to the father custodian of New Mexico, Fray Alonso de Benavides. And the blessed Mother tells of having been frequently to New Mexico and to the Grand Quivira, adding that eastward from the Grand Quivira are situated the kingdoms of Ticlas, Theas, and Caburcol. She also says that these names are not the ones belonging to those kingdoms, but come close to the real names.*[9]

Father Massanet continues to write how he had wanted to find out whether any Frenchmen were there and that he had been told by an Indian whom he had converted and now possessed a high degree of truthfulness that there were indeed Frenchmen living to the north. Massanet seems to have been as eager as de León for their expulsion from the Spanish frontier.

This group set out in March 1689, three months after the French colony had been overrun and destroyed. The entrada, with the help of Géry, whose memory of location seemed to improve the nearer they came to La Salle's site, did locate the grotesque remains, three weeks after setting out, on April 22, 1689. De León's accounting of the scene of the ruins is as blithe as is Massanet's:

> *Having halted with the forces about an arquebus-shot away, we went to see it, and found all the houses sacked, all the chests, bottle-cases, and all the rest of the settlers' furniture broken; apparently more than two hundred*

*books, torn apart, and with the rotten leaves scattered through the patios—
all in French. We noted that the perpetrators of this massacre had pulled
everything [the colonists] had out of their chests, and divided the booty
among themselves; and what they had not cared for they had torn to pieces,
making a frightful sack of all the French possessed.... We found three dead
bodies scattered over the plain. One of these, from the dress that still clung to
the bones, appeared to be that of a woman. We took the bodies up, chanted
mass with the bodies present, and buried them.*[10]

This sure proof of the French encroachment into Spanish territory was
cause for much concern. Not only had La Salle's venture been proven, but
the natives declared that others still inhabited the territory, living among the
native peoples. In fact, this excursion had produced two French survivors of
La Salle's enterprise; they returned to Mexico with Massanet and de León.
(There were a few other Frenchmen who chose to stay with the Indians of
the Hasinai confederacy rather than risk imprisonment with the Spanish.)
Nevertheless, this persistent French shade cloaking the Spanish frontier
guaranteed the Spanish government's support for any future efforts by the
Franciscans to found missions in the region. And Father Massanet was not
about to let this opportunity slip away. In this manner, the colonization of
Tejas was realized.

When the viceroy Conde de Galve heard of the French settlement, Fray
Massanet wasted little time in expounding his theory that the Indians of the
region were ready and eager souls for conversion. With reports from both
this Franciscan and de León, the viceroy chose to redeploy a contingent of
Spanish men to the area, this time with the goal of founding a permanent
settlement in the area. After having convened a *junta* and a decision having
been reached, this new entrada set out from Monclova in March 1690. Again
led by de León, with Fray Massanet and 3 other religious, Father Francisco
de Jesús María Casañas among them, this expedition of 110 soldiers, with
sundries for both the military and religious, considered itself prepared for
the harsh realities of the Texas frontier.

The expedition crossed the Rio Grande at a point by then referred to as
Paso de Francia and traveled northeast, returning to the site of La Salle's
ruined colony. Massanet, evidently still enraged by the temerity of the French
to encroach on Spanish lands, torched the remains of the French settlement
himself. Relieved of this, the entrada continued into the Hasinai territories,
where they found and retrieved two members of La Salle's colony: Pierre
Meunier, now age twenty; and Pierre Talon, age fourteen. Meunier had

been in the group of seventeen on La Salle's last scouting mission, had seen the massacre and decided to remain with the Indians rather than continue on with a retinue of murderers. Talon, barely into puberty when La Salle left Fort St. Louis the last time, had been taken captive by the Karankawa after the fort's destruction. Both now bore the facial tattoos of the natives and, somewhat surprisingly, were more than hesitant to accompany the Spanish back to New Spain. These men accompanied the entrada to the Hasinai and served as interpreters for the Spanish.

In May of the same year, this expedition reached the Nabedaches tribe and decided to found the first mission in east Texas there, near the Neches River. The area on which to build the mission was chosen on May 22. By May 24, the members of the expedition had constructed a wooden chapel in which Mass was conducted, and the Spanish flag was raised. During the next several days, the soldiers and Indians together constructed a colony of several buildings, creating some semblance of order where for millennia had been only wilderness. They named this mission San Francisco de los Tejas, in conjoined honor of the pater familias of the Franciscan Order and the natives among whom they settled. Father Massanet was handed official possession of the mission on June 1.

The following day, Massanet left with de León to return to Coahuila. Fray Francisco Casañas de Jesús María and the remaining two friars were left behind to tend to the mission. The group had been stationary only a couple of weeks, but already the natives were complaining to de León about the lewd behavior of some of his men. Evidently, just before the entrada had left Monclova, de León found he was 20 men short of his assigned 110 soldiers. He had hurriedly assembled a contingent from Coahuila to make up the shortcoming, but this was an eclectic group, "composed chiefly of shoemakers, masons, tailors, miners and adventurers—a motley, incoherent group inspired by selfish motives and foredooming to failure the enterprise."[11] Many of these found great opportunity for prurient and licentious behavior in the woods of east Texas. To add further injury to the situation, when the group was preparing to leave in late May, de León wanted to leave 50 soldiers with the friars. But Massanet, fearing that such a martial presence would intimidate the natives, demanded that only 3 soldiers needed to remain. The quarrel ended in the latter's favor, but between his men's misbehavior and the arguments with Massanet, de León was soon relieved of duty when the party finally reached New Spain. Nonetheless, during the trek back to the Mexican interior, de León did hear of a few more French survivors in the area of the Gulf Coast. These were none other than the other 3 Talon children—Robert, Lucien and Marie—who had been among the Karankawa tribe and, like their brother Pierre, had been branded with the tattoos of the natives on their faces and bodies. When they had come to New Spain, all the children were placed in the care of Viceroy Gaspar de la Cerda Sandoval Silva y Mendoza, Conde de Galve.

The viceroy, after receiving the reports from de León and Massanet, decided to redeploy Spanish efforts to the same region. Granted royal permission to proceed with this expedition, El Conde de Galve prepared for the new enterprise with better planning and support than before. As always, the purpose was twofold: the first, to proffer support to the existing mission; the second, of course, to establish a stronger Spanish presence along this frontier. To that end, the viceroy implemented a different stratagem; this entrada would be headed by Don Domingo Terán de los Rios, the new governor of Coahuila and Texas, who was to make his entrada with fifty soldiers. Additionally, forty more were to be sent by sea to lend more assured support by arriving at Espíritu Santo Bay. Obviously, the political situation was of greater value than the ecclesiastical one. However, the viceroy understood that pacifying the indigenous tribes of this region, as compared to those that Cortés had encountered, required more Bibles than bullets.

This entrada called for the settlement of eight new missions in east Texas. Again, Father Massanet was given the task of overseeing the religious component. To this end, he employed fourteen friars and several laypersons and ensured that all were well supplied with the provisions and victuals that would be needed once these missions were left to operate on their own. Governor Terán and company departed from Presidio de San Francisco de Coahuila on May 16, 1691, and joined with Father Massanet's entourage four days later.

This entrada, while following the same route to the Rio Grande, and most likely crossing it again at the Paso de Francia, decided to try a dissimilar but more direct trail toward the Tejas region. The group crossed and recrossed rivers and streams that, while the same ones other entradas had reached, were so unfamiliar at their junctures as to continually be acquiring new names. As Walter McCaleb notes, "In the course of time it became practically impossible to identify a place by its name, for the same name probably had been applied to several other points."[12]

Within a couple of weeks, after being delayed by severe weather, the Spanish were met by a small group of Indians carrying letters from the mission in east Texas. The news was not good. Disease (most likely smallpox) had decimated those at the mission, including one of the religious. The crops were failing, and the livestock were dying. Terán decided to dispatch twenty of his group to the bay of Espíritu Santo in an effort to locate their naval resources. Once this company reached the shore, no sign of the ships was to be seen. The small contingent left a note with the coastal tribe to deliver to the ship's commander should he arrive. It was, however, during their trek back to the Neches that they ransomed Jean Baptiste Talon and Eustache Breman, two of the children taken by the Karankawa after wasting La Salle's colony.

The group now rejoined, Massanet and Terán argued about how to proceed. Terán was mostly concerned with scouting deeper into the Caddoan territory; Massanet obviously had the welfare of the mission and its people at heart. Terán, still desirous of the supplies adrift somewhere in the gulf, called for a smaller unit of soldiers to return there. Massanet maintained that the entire enterprise should continue on to the mission, since it was clearly in a precarious situation. The latter's opinion held, and the group continued to the mission. The religious, however, more eager than the military to reach the despairing mission, traveled ahead in order to make contact as soon as possible.

Father de Jesús María greeted the group with news worse than imagined. Not only had Fray Fonte Cubierta passed away, but both season's crops had failed to take root, much of the cattle had also died and, worse still, the same epidemic that had martyred Cubierta had claimed three hundred of the Hasinais and over three thousand of the various tribes of the Tejas. The newly arrived group also learned, however, that Father de Jesús María had constructed another mission in the intervening time, Mission Santísimo Nombre de María, and that the religious, despite their worldly buffetings, had managed still to realize some of their celestial duties by baptizing close to one hundred natives. This was almost the totality of the friars' success, though. According to Father María, the persistence of the epidemic had led many of the Indians to wonder if the Spanish and their holy water were not the cause of the disease and begin plotting revenge. Father María gave two reasons as to how he staved off the Indians' hostilities. Primarily, he argued that, while the natives became ill, Fray Cubierta had also succumbed to the same. Next, when the chief of nine Tejas tribes, Xinesi, became ill, Father María baptized him on what appeared at the time to be his deathbed. The chief recovered, "became a very good Christian" and mollified temperaments for some time. Nevertheless, Fray María stated that what really instigated the emotional turmoil among the natives was the lack of gifts. It appears that as resources withered, resentment grew.

This was the situation Terán found when he arrived in August 1691. By all accounts, all were very glad of his arrival—the religious for the obvious reasons and the natives because the governor had brought more tokens and gifts. In total, Mission San Francisco de los Tejas had been striving alone for fourteen months.

Proceeding to plan, Terán declared the Tejas territory for Spain and applied the name of El Nuevo Reyno de de Nueva Montaña de Santander y Santillana. Next, after delivering the remainder of the resources (animals, provisions, et cetera), Terán left for a return to the bay to search for the naval contingent near the end of August, leaving the religious to their work at the mission. Terán located the small fleet on September 8. It had made landfall in early July, but for whatever reason, the earlier scouting party had failed to find it. For just over two weeks the group waited for the supplies to be unloaded. Again reunited, the expedition set out for the missions of east Texas in late September.

Due to the autumn weather, Terán and his group were delayed. They waited for swollen rivers and creeks to recede and for mud-clogged roads to dry. It was two months before they arrived back at the missions on October 26. But Terán was impatient to continue with his orders. After resting at the missions for only a week, he again wanted to reconnoiter the territories of the Cadodaches. They set out ill prepared and ill tempered, Father Massanet among them. Most historians agree that Terán's decision to begin this effort during winter was made solely due to his preoccupation with wanting to be done with the venture. Undoubtedly this is true. After finding the Red River, the border of the Caddoan territory, Terán found a canoe, made a couple of lighthearted attempts at soundings and sketches of the river's path and allowed Massanet across to find whether the natives might be willing conversos. The whole company then started back for the two missions.

Once back, the tensions between the two leaders did not end. Terán said he needed fresh horses and a few beef for his journey to the coast, where he would meet the supply ships and sail back to New Spain. Massanet declined, saying that the religious needed them at the missions. Terán told his soldiers to take what they needed, and they did. Among the small contingent of soldiers left to protect the friars in their work, the lewd behavior only increased after their commander's departure. Of the crops that the religious tried to establish, two years of drought took care of all but some corn. Of the friars' attitudes at being left to fend for themselves in the wilderness, one can only imagine the incredible burden such a thing would exert on the mind. After Terán, the Indians only became more unruly. They did not take to the idea of confinement within the missions' walls. The cattle became infected with some illness, and most perished. Even a small relief party in the summer of 1693 could not deliver enough confidence to assuage the temperaments on either side of the missions' walls. In fact, several of the religious took the opportunity to return to Coahuila with the relief party rather than stay with the missions. Soon after, Massanet asked the viceroy for more supplies, but the latter was not inclined to help. Tensions with the French had subsided, but the efforts to mollify the region so far had met with little success. In August 1693, the missions were ordered abandoned. So, on October 25, the last of the friars, after burying their aspirations, the missions' bells and whatever else they could not carry, departed for New Spain. For them, who had trained for this, their life's work, the abandoning of what they had built with their own hands must have been devastating. To prevent any desecration to the mission, Massanet put it to the torch before leaving.

As to the causes of this protracted failure, it is easy enough to surmise that a confluence of events brought the enterprise down. As Clark wrote over a century ago:

> *The missionary plan (of constructing the eight missions) seems to have been abandoned entirely; and the missions already established were not in a flourishing condition. The friendliness of the Tejas was not unmixed with duplicity; while professing good will in order to secure the presents which the Spaniards frequently made them, they were constantly pilfering from the missions and stealing and killing the animals. Moreover, they attributed the disease and deaths among them to the influence of the new religion which they had professed, and began to rebel against it and to threaten the priests. These difficulties were aggravated by the harshness and lack of tact which marked the dealings of the soldiers with the natives.*[13]

Inauspicious as the end was, this chapter of the Franciscans' history in Texas serves at least to illustrate the fortitude and faith of a group of men willing to leap into the unknown for the furtherance of their beliefs; at best, their efforts demonstrate a profound dedication to their order, coupled with a perseverance that few have shown throughout history. Even though twenty years would elapse between this attempt and the next, the friars' determination would ultimately shape Texas into the region as it is known today.

CHAPTER 2

THE MISSIONS AND PRESIDIOS OF GOLIAD

The presidio Nuestra Señora de Loreto, today more commonly referred to as La Bahía ("the Bay"), was founded in April 1721. Constructed on the site of La Salle's Fort St. Louis, this garrison was built on the very ground where Father Massanet had razed the French colony just thirty years prior. This endeavor would also include, after one more year, the Nuestra Señora del Espíritu Santo de Zúñiga Mission and then, approximately thirty years later, the Nuestra Señora del Rosario Mission. As with so many of the Spanish missions in Texas, the first two mentioned here, now in Goliad, had their origins elsewhere. Many of the missions were moved or transferred from one location to another for either political reasons or as attempts to regain contact with or retreat from particular Indian tribes. At other times, the original locations were simply deemed too lacking in resources.

From the Franciscans' retreat from the first missions in east Texas in 1693, they had continued their efforts to persuade the government in New Spain for more excursions to reclaim what they perceived as lost. Their requests were continually refused for a number of years. However, just as Father Massanet had persevered for as long as he could at San Francisco de los Tejas (Santísimo Nombre de María had been carried off by a raging Neches River), even he eventually became distraught and left. As John Kessell notes, "Having lived among the Hasinais, he [Massanet] now had nothing good to say about them. Insolent, deceitful, hopelessly idolatrous, constantly plotting to murder their missionaries, interested only in material benefits, and unwilling to congregate in mission towns, these Natives would have to be forced to convert."[14] Spanish interest in the region had waned. There did remain one, at least, who, even returning to Monclova with Massanet and the others, continued in his efforts to reach and preach to the Indians of the Tejas territory. It would be this young priest's ardor that would eventually result in the missions that are today at Goliad.

Francisco Hidalgo had joined the Franciscans at the age of fifteen and then crossed to New Spain, with Massanet and the others, when he was only in his early twenties. From the time the missionaries returned to Monclova in 1694, Fray Hidalgo continued to reach out to the natives in and around the Rio Grande areas. In 1700, Hidalgo was instrumental in establishing San Juan Bautista Mission just a few miles below the Rio Grande, a mission that came to serve as a sort of oasis in the desert between the civilizations in New Spain and the wilds north of the river.

After a few frustrating years trying to acquire the resources for another mission effort into Texas, Father Hidalgo came upon a plan he suspected would entertain rather than depress the government of New Spain. Realizing that evangelical philosophies were not resonating with the officials, he decided that a political motivation would capture the necessary attentions. He was right. Hidalgo, like the Spanish government, knew that the territory of Louisiana was being settled successfully by the French. In 1711, having spent the past fifteen years at Mission San Juan Bautista agitatedly trying to conjure a plan for a return to the Tejas, Fray Hidalgo wrote a letter to the governor of Louisiana, Antoine de La Mothe, Sieur de Cadillac, asking for help in re-founding missions in east Texas. In his earnestness, Hidalgo made three copies and had each carried in a different direction. Then, having waited two years, he retired to the College at Querétaro in 1712. He did not learn of his success until 1714, when news finally reached him at the colegio. Even then, he could never have known just how successful he had been.

Some have written that Cadillac ignored the offer at first. Robert Weddle states that Cadillac "set immediately upon his task of establishing

Signature of Father Francisco Hidalgo. *Courtesy of the Catholic Archives at San Antonio. Not to be reproduced without the proper authorization of the archives.*

trade with Mexico by sending a merchandise ship to Veracruz, offering a trade for livestock and other necessities. But Spanish officials turned the ship back with a stern warning that the ports of New Spain were closed to all foreign commerce."[15] Still, with his interest piqued, Cadillac dispatched one Juchereau de St. Denis to Texas to establish trade relations with the native populace, the Hasinai confederacy, and to locate the letter's Franciscan author. St. Denis complied and was extremely successful in establishing relations with the Tejas. He soon learned their language and became a welcomed visitor and trader. Two years later, in 1713, Cadillac ventured further; he ordered St. Denis to visit the Spanish mission in Coahuila, namely San Juan Bautista, ostensibly to establish trade relations. Depending on the source, St. Denis is described variously as gregarious, flamboyant, kindly and romantic. Whatever the truth of his character, one thing is certain—he was quickly accepted by whomever he dealt with. While traveling toward New Spain, Denis acquired a companion, a Chief Bernardino of the Tejas, and together they entered San Juan Bautista Mission. The captain of the outpost, Diego Ramón, promptly arrested the Frenchman and, after a few hours of conversation, had Denis imprisoned…in his own home. St. Denis's imprisonment lasted a few weeks while Ramón waited to hear from his superiors, with the former's only real confinement being the interior of the presidio. During this time, St. Denis and Ramón wrote to Father Hidalgo at Querétaro, making mention of hopes for another entrada into the region Hidalgo was so eager to return to. In fact, conditions at the mission became so comfortable while all waited for word from the Mexican capital that St. Denis had time to court and marry the granddaughter of Diego Ramón, Manuela Sánchez.

Rumor, in its peculiar fashion of both passing through any barrier and remaining where it has fled, had already reached the ears of the viceroy of New Spain: the French had begun trading with the Hasinai tribes. Accordingly, when Ramón's letter reached the capital (it had been his duty to declare St. Denis's arrival at the mission), the authorities did lead Denis away in chains to the Mexican capital for interrogation. Domingo Ramón accompanied the soldiers, most probably to plead St. Denis's case. For several weeks, the junta general listened to St. Denis's explanations. In the end, Hidalgo's letter and ambitions were approved. The authorities had before them a Frenchman who, although potentially adversarial, was nonetheless useful as a guide and translator. His charm also garnered him the role of commissary official for the expedition. The junta decided that Denis could well be an asset for another Spanish entrada into a territory so ashamedly abandoned twenty years before. Domingo Ramón, son of Diego, would lead the Spanish soldiers, and St. Denis would accompany him. This entrada was multipurposed. The Spanish felt the need to expel the ever-threatening French, reestablish those missions abandoned earlier with even more and pursue those natives who had been harassing Spanish interests for the past several years in the regions that lay near the Rio Grande and to the north. In addition to twenty-five soldiers, several Spanish families were incorporated into the group. In fact, just as the friars had been requesting, seven married soldiers brought along their families, the wives of whom are considered the first Spanish women in the region of Texas. Ten Franciscans from the Colegio de Querétaro and their ancillary laymen would join the unit. Within this religious group was Father Hidalgo. Combined with these were three friars from the newer missionary college at Zacatecas. Including the soldiers, Spanish civilians, religious, Indian auxiliaries and slaves, the total number of the group was near one hundred. The beasts of burden and baggage accrued was expansive by contemporary standards. It appears the Spanish had learned at least one lesson in their previous experience: bring enough gifts to keep everyone pacified for a prolonged period. This expedition left Saltillo (today the capital of the state of Coahuila) in February 1716 and reached the Rio Grande by April.

On June 22, the expedition came to the Trinity River (at the time called Rio de San Juan Bautista), within reach of the Hasinai tribes. By early July, the expedition's members had founded the Nuestro Padre San Francisco de los Tejas Mission, just twelve miles, or four leagues (a league being the distance one could walk in an hour, roughly three miles), from the original San Francisco de los Tejas Mission. Father Isidoro Felix de Espinosa, the president of the Querétaro college, was given official charge of the new mission. In turn, he transferred care to Fray Hidalgo. In short order, three more missions were established by this group, the next being Nuestra Señora de la Purísima Concepción de los Hasinais Mission, founded

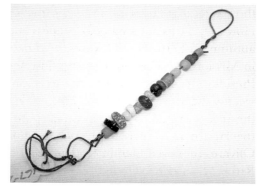

Spanish trade beads from Mission Rosario. *Courtesy of Texas Archaeological Research Laboratory.*

about twenty miles to the northeast of San Francisco near what is today Douglass, Texas. Fray Gabriel de Vergara was given charge of this mission, and Father Espinosa chose the site as his headquarters.

Next, Nuestra Señora de Guadalupe was established about nine leagues east of Concepción. (If one considers a couple of these missions situated in present-day Louisiana, they would be correct.) Fray Margil de Jesús was given charge of this mission. He was the same friar who, in 1707, had founded the College of Nuestra Señora de Guadalupe de Zacatecas.

The fourth mission, San Jose de los Nazonis, was constructed approximately five leagues southeast of Concepción. This mission was placed in the care of Father Benito Sanchez. Almost immediately, the Spanish realized they had overextended their reach. The missions themselves were within relatively friendly territory, but just to the north and west hostile Apache tribes threatened Spaniard and Tejas tribes alike. To the south, the cannibalistic Karankawa clutched onto the region through which any incoming supplies or retreat excursions would pass. To fortify their positions, St. Denis and Ramón, accompanied by Father Margil de Jesús, traveled into the French regions (Mobile) later in 1716. After their return, two more missions, Nuestra Señora de los Dolores and San Miguel de Linares de los Adaes, were established early in 1717, the former near present-day San Augustine, Texas, and the latter near Robeline, Louisiana. Fray Margil de Jesús was put in charge of these. Still, these two other missions did little by way of strengthening a tenuous position. Shortly before the trek to Mobile, the friars and Ramón had dictated a letter to the viceroy asking for more soldiers, an increase in their pay and more donatives for the natives.

These restored missions enjoyed early successes. Hundreds if not thousands of natives came to the missions for instruction and resources. However, it was not long before illness and deprivations began again. In the autumn of 1716, Fray Olivares, who had decided to remain at the border in Mission San Francisco Solano (just across the Rio Grande from today's Presidio, Texas), traveled to the Mexican capital to consult with the new viceroy, Marques de Valero. He proffered a report on the condition of the recent entrada. More missions were needed, Olivares stated, because the French were increasing both in number and commerce. In addition, Olivares proposed planting an entirely new settlement on the San Antonio River. Olivares's extended report would ultimately lead to an expedition, led by Martín de Alarcón, that would reestablish the Mission San Francisco Solano (located near Mission San Juan Bautista in Coahuila) to that of Mission San Antonio de Valero, along with presidio San Antonio de Béxar, which together would be termed Villa de Bejar. This area would become the nucleus for most of the future expeditions, the fortified center within the Texas territory, effectively replacing San Juan Bautista as the depot for all mission work within Texas. In all probability, this had been Olivares's plan all along. Alarcón's expedition, however, was also supposed to resupply those missions newly founded in the east. In that regard, he failed. Those missions were floundering. Again the crops were not producing, again illness spread among the religious and Indians and again what resources had been stored were depleted. With the loss of resources came the loss of the indigenous populace. As Eleanor Buckley explains, "Urgent requests for alleviation were sent to the home government both before and after Alarcón's expedition, but for various reasons no relief came."[16] These new missions in the Tejas region would prevail, very weakly, for nearly two years while awaiting word and supplies. Indeed, one supply entrada, leaving in December 1717, was headed by Fray Miguel Nuñez de Haro. This group, finding the rivers too swollen to cross with all their supplies, made its riparian nests and tried to wait for the waters to recede. By the end of March, Nuñez was forced to retreat. He and his small contingent had tried to outlast the season, but nature proved a more tenacious opponent. Accordingly, Father Nuñez chose to leave the cache half hidden under a group of trees, using his tent as cover, and then sent a note ahead by Indian courier to the missions' friars. Father Nuñez prayed both that the couriers would not read the note and take the latent supplies themselves and that they would not take so long that the needy friars never located the stash. Nearly four months later, the letter reached the religious in the missions of east Texas, and within a couple of weeks they had found the supplies exactly where the faded letter indicated. The religious among the Tejas learned much from the letters. Until that time, they had been unaware that Martín de Alarcón had been named governor of Coahuila and Texas and that he, in conjunction with Father Olivares, had begun a new Spanish settlement on the San Antonio River, a project that could cut in half the distance and time needed to resupply their own or future missions.

Meanwhile, the friars at the east Texas missions, according to their records, had been true to their order. Where lesser men might have retreated, these men stayed with little to no provisions. According to their reports, they had no wine for sacraments, no wax for their candles, their clothing was literally falling to shreds and they had to settle on shooting crows for a source of meat. After reading the letters, the friars learned that there had been orders given to Alarcón for the health and maintenance of the missions. The only difficulty was that the orders were two years old. What, exactly, had Alarcón been

Interior of Nuestra Señora de Loreto/La Bahía. *Image courtesy of Angie Browne.*

doing? According to the writings, Alarcón had left for the Tejas missions with replacement soldiers (most had deserted), grain, cattle and other sundries. Since the orders were two years old, the friars met to discuss what to do. The supplies left by Nuñez would only slightly and temporarily assuage the depth of the cavity; something had to be done to prevent certain future decay. The friars met at Mission de los Dolores. (This was a most suitable place to meet under the circumstances; surely this did not go unnoticed by the friars.) They decided that a friar from each colegio, one from Zacatecas and one from Querétaro, should leave to meet with the viceroy and explain the true nature of the situation at their missions. Fathers Espinosa and Matías Sáenz de San Antonio were selected. At San Antonio de Padua, an area in the same region of Villa de Bejar, Fray Espinosa understood that Alarcón had left, first for Espíritu Santo Bay and afterward scheduled for the missions in the east. He decided to await Alarcón at the bay and gave his letters to Friar Sáenz, who continued on toward the Mexican capital.

In June 1718, the viceroy discussed the situation at the eastern missions before another junta. Father Sáenz could not have known that Captain Ramón, having received word of Nuñez's failure, had already sent his own letter to the Mexican capital attesting to the same predicament. The commission allotted another four thousand pesos for the missions in the east. Still, after reaching the viceroy in November 1718, Sáenz read his letters, heavy in their grave optimism, a burden that he had carried for so many miles. He complained of the bitter environment and lack of support. Nevertheless, with most of the Franciscans' concerns all but brushed aside, Sáenz left New Spain in February 1719 having grown tired of waiting for a thick bureaucracy to soften into action.

Ruins of Mission Nuestra Señora del Rosario. *Image courtesy of author.*

For some time, circumstances remained as they had for two years. Provisions of all sorts were beyond scarce, and the French, who were settling in comfortably only a few leagues to the east, were running a brisk business with the natives, swapping guns for horses. Father Espinosa did, however, meet up with Governor Alarcón's train at Espíritu Santo and directed him back to the missions in the east. One can only guess what the initial conversations were like, but Espinosa's accounting of the event after the governor's departure leaves little room for doubt as to the tenor. He wrote soon after the governor's party had left, "The Texas missions remained just as they were before, and the governor returned to Coahuila without having given any favorable directions [*providencia*] for the missions' growth."[17] It was all in vain, however, as political events would, once again, test the mettle of the Franciscans' resolve.

Early in 1719, France and Spain were once again at war. By autumn, the Spanish outpost of Pensacola had been taken, and by reports, one hundred French soldiers were marching toward east Texas. However, news of this was slow reaching Texas; not until summer of the same year did the French commander at Natchitoches, Philippe Blondel, understand that he was to be hostile toward the Spanish missionaries just to his west. So informed, Blondel "attacked" Mission San Miguel with a force of seven men and found the mission garrisoned by two men: one a Spanish soldier, the other a Franciscan brother. This lay brother was able to steal away into the woods and escape to Mission Nuestra Señora de los Dolores while the French were pilfering San Miguel. Blondel grabbed what was available (next to nothing) and then raided the henhouse. The mistake was not so much stealing the friar's food as tying the live chickens to his own horse. The chickens' flitting and squawking caused the horse to rear and bolt Blondel onto the dirt; thus, the infamous "Chicken War" of 1719. It is difficult to fathom that such an anemic and pitiful aggression should have had the result that it did. With the sole Spanish soldier arrested, the Franciscan brother reached Frays Espinosa and Margil to report the event. These two in turn wrote several letters, which were sent hurriedly to San Antonio, the viceroy and the missions just across the Rio Grande. Meanwhile, Espinosa, Margil and others took refuge in nearby Mission Concepción. The soldiers at the presidio were ready to withdraw. All of the Spanish were aware that the Indians now carried French rifles. The result of another conflict was now not a sure Spanish victory. There was every reason to believe that the French might make confederates of the natives and that the fight would be hopelessly one-sided, with the Spanish besieged and alone within their empty missions. Captain Ramón

Painting of St. Veronica at La Bahía. *Image courtesy of author.*

was all for retreating toward San Antonio; Fathers Margil and Espinosa wanted to remain at the missions, as was their duty. The eight wives of the soldiers of the presidio sided with Ramón—all wanted desperately to be out of the wilderness and away from the occult threat. As Espinosa wrote at the time, "Everything was confusion and sadness."[18]

At a meeting of Ramón, Espinosa, Margil and the other Franciscans, the decision was made to leave Mission San Antonio de los Tejas. Ramón, soldiers, wives and all others would retreat to the borders of the Tejas and wait. Espinosa and Margil returned to Concepción to mollify the Indians' concerns over the Spaniards' leaving. These two remained two months before learning that Ramón was pressing on deeper and closer toward Bexar. Espinosa and Margil had no choice but to follow them; again, the east was abandoned.

Before leaving this time, Espinosa and Magril wrote other letters to the viceroy with detailed complaints about why and how all of this had occurred. As Buckley observes, "The missionaries attributed their inability to resist the present hostile movement to the general failure of the government to properly support them, and, in particular, to the failure of Alarcón to follow his instructions."[19]

Spain's answer to all this confusion and sadness was to replace Alarcón. Marqués de San Miguel de Aguayo was appointed governor and general of the provinces of Coahuila, the New Philippines and Texas in 1719. Maybe not surprisingly, but certainly presciently, the year before, Spain's king had issued a royal *cédula* maintaining that "no French ships be allowed in any Spanish port; and charged the viceroy to exert himself to supply and maintain the Texas missions, and to place the greatest number of missionaries at San Antonio, on account of its being the nearest settlement to Espíritu Santo." He ordered that at the latter place there should be erected a fort, on the spot where La Salle's had been.[20] With this directive, Aguayo, accompanied by Father Margil, began his expedition to reoccupy east Texas. Although delayed, to Espinosa's dismay, for a year and a half, the expedition (consisting of five hundred soldiers and all necessary ancillaries) progressed through San Juan Bautista in December 1720. Domingo Ramón, son of Diego, who had been at the San Antonio presidio since retreating from east Texas the previous year, was ordered by Aguayo to proceed to La Bahía with a detachment of forty men and occupy that region as a coastal defense.

Aguayo's expedition was heavily supplied. It took almost three months for the entire train to cross the Rio Grande; the quantity of cattle, sheep, horses, clothing and supplies was immense, according to the expedition's diarist, Father Juan Antonio de la Peña. By mid-March 1721, all were crossed and marching toward San Antonio via the Camino Real. Along the journey, Aguayo was notified that the omnipresent St. Denis had filled the vacuum left by the Spanish in east Texas. Aguayo sent notice of a truce, since the two countries had already done so, and St. Denis and his men agreed to withdraw to Natchitoches, allowing Aguayo to reestablish six missions and a

Spanish artifacts from Mission Rosario: key and candle tool. *Courtesy of Texas Archaeological Research Laboratory.*

presidio in east Texas. Aguayo added the presidio Nuestra Señora del Pilar de los Adaes in the region as an extra impediment to French encroachment.

Having met up with Ramón's detachment later at La Bahía, they constructed the Nuestra Señora de Loreto Presidio on the site of La Salle's former colony. Approximately one year later, the group founded Mission Nuestra Señora del Espíritu Santo de Zuñiga among the Karankawa Indians. The new mission was given to the care of those Franciscans of the college at Zacatecas. Its name paid homage to both the old site and the viceroy of New Spain, Báltasar de Zuñiga. *La Bahía* was the term used to identify the Spanish settlements in the area. It was considered, along with the re-founded Mission San Miguel de los Adaes (which would serve as the capital of Texas in later years) in eastern Texas, in need of the strongest fortifications against any French, English or native threat. Aguayo placed Don Domingo Ramón in charge of the presidio at La Bahía, and Father Agustín Patrón y Guzmán had care of the mission.

The Aguayo expedition had succeeded beyond expectations. Where before the Chicken War there had been only a few missions in the east, there now stood ten. Four presidios watched over these missions, rather than the two previous, and in these were garrisoned a total of 268 soldiers, as opposed to the paltry 50 or so, as before. Again, as Buckley observes of the Aguayo entrada, "It was perhaps the most ably executed of all the expeditions that entered Texas, and in results it was doubtless the most important. It secured to Spain her hold on Texas for about one hundred and fifteen years."[21] Regretfully, when Aguayo retired from Texas, it seems that so, too, did the Spanish fortunes. Soon, the name "Ramón" would again be a catalyst for distress.

La Bahía, today's Matagorda Bay area, was not long content with success. Aguayo had left Texas in 1722, arriving back in Coahuila in May. Diego Ramón, now elderly but still in command at the "Gateway to Texas," the Mission San Juan Bautista, did not know at the time, but he was to be relieved of his duties. The Spanish crown had found fault with his amicable attitude toward the French in general and St. Denis in particular. The king issued a royal decree that would dismiss Ramón to some further outpost, blunting his ability to communicate with the French. St. Denis and his Spanish wife were also to be removed to distant Guatemala. Both bits of information the elder Ramón never learned, because his death was hastened by more troubling personal news. His son Domingo was the instigator of another Spanish atrocity against a native population whose bodies they were supposed to be guarding and whose souls they should have been saving.

Façade of Mission Nuestra Señora del Espíritu Santo/La Bahía. *Image courtesy of author.*

Only a year and a half after its founding, La Bahía was in trouble. The tragic story began on December 15, 1723, when an Indian from the mission asked for some food at the home of one of the soldiers at the presidio Nuestra Señora de Loreto. This Indian had the unfortunate idea of shaking his blanket out inside the apartment while he waited for his beef. The soldier's wife, grinding some corn in the same area, became incredulous at what she perceived as the native's barbarous manners. She called to her husband, who threw the native out of the home. This incident, at first a flash of bigotry, flamed into a riot that perhaps a better man could have tempered. But Ramón, angered at the Indians' insolence, ordered what natives he could locate arrested and confined in a small room at the presidio. His plan was to hang them all, making examples of them. The crowd, sensing the approaching violence, decided to make a break for it, and Ramón ordered his men to attack. In the mêlée, Ramón was stabbed in the chest by a native with a pair of scissors. Incensed and driven to desperation, Ramón ordered a cannon shot fired directly into the holding cell. This gave the Indians a means of escape, save a single native woman who was seized and hanged soon afterward. Don Domingo, wounded bodily and in stature, died eight days later, on December 23.

Domingo Ramón was replaced by his son Diego, named for his grandfather. From all accounts, Diego continued in his father's infamous ways. He had no command of the region. As Weddle points out, "An official investigation of goings on at the presidio resulted in formal charges of negligence being brought against him. Gambling was rampant at the post; the soldiers were in rags, their arms unfit for service; discipline was nonexistent."[22] As a result, Diego was soon replaced by Juan Antonio de Bustillo y Ceballos. However, this changing of the guard could not undo the damage. The Franciscans complained to their superiors that the Karankawa would not settle within the mission, nor did they take to the Catholic faith as readily as hoped. There were several instances of deprivations of supplies and random violence on each side. Finally, by 1726, the decision was made to relocate La Bahía, both mission and presidio, approximately thirty miles farther inland, nearer the Guadalupe River in today's Victoria County, also referred to now as "Mission Valley."

This new effort was much more successful. The Franciscans now attended to the Tamique and Aranama Indian tribes. While the religious continued to have problems with the natives adjusting to what they considered confinement, nevertheless, the mission's work flourished. Dams were built and rock *acequias* (aqueducts) nourished the surrounding fields. Additionally, the neighboring *rancheria* produced more cattle than the immediate area needed; some of the supplies were exported both to the missions in the east and the San Antonio region. For twenty-six years, the Franciscans' work yielded the results they had expected; hundreds of Indians were baptized and converted to Catholicism. As became the custom, the Franciscans encouraged the disparate Indian groups to intermarry in an effort to pacify intertribal fighting. Those natives who chose to become members of the mission community were also allowed to participate in their own governance. The Franciscans began a system of custodial care whereby some of the Indians were elected to oversee certain elements of daily life. While this has been seen by some as an attempt to westernize the Indians, the Franciscans simply viewed it as work to guide the *gentiles* toward salvation. For a while at least, La Bahía appeared to be functioning as intended. Spain, however, was not the only European country to realize the gains to be had from the territory. The French and English also recognized that broad reaches of land, from present-day Tamaulipas to the lower side of the Rio Grande Valley, still lay open to exploration and settlement. Someone needed to claim it quickly.

The mission San Juan Bautista had, for many years, been the gateway through which most every Spanish entrada had progressed to the Paso de Francia. In 1745, a small contingent of soldiers from the mission discovered another crossing point farther to the east. It was named Paso de Jacinto, after the platoon's commander, Jacinto de León. This new crossing point was to become the door that opened onto this region of southeastern Texas.

The Spanish government in 1746 employed José de Escandón, a sergeant major at Querétaro and seasoned soldier in the Indian wars within Seno Mexico—the middle, or "breast" of Mexico—to explore and settle this region. (Escandón would later be called the "Exterminator of the Pames [Indians] of Querétaro.") The assignment was undertaken vigorously, as Weddle noted: "Escandón approached the problem of exploration and colonization as he would a military campaign. His plan was to penetrate the area from seven different points at the same time, all the expeditions converging at the mouth of the Rio Grande."[23] Escandón proceeded with his task energetically and with little patience for anyone who impeded the plan's completion. When one contingent of his seven failed to rendezvous at the appropriate time, Escandón dismissed their commander, noting that another had made a similar journey and had faced similar hardships but had still managed to fulfill his assignment.

Reconstruction at La Bahía, 1930s. *Courtesy of Texas Parks and Wildlife Department.*

The Escandón expedition was as successful as Aguayo's had been twenty-six years earlier. The distinction was that, while the successes of Aguayo were for the Franciscans, those of Escandón were financial. The enormous territory Escandón claimed, from Tampico to the San Antonio River in south central Texas, was labeled Nuevo Santander, after his native city in Spain. It was during his mapping of this area that Escandón proposed the idea of transferring the mission and presidio at La Bahía to their present site along the San Antonio River basin (although Wakefield suggests that the transfer was at the request of the missionaries). After proffering the plan to the government, the decision was made to accept Escandón's proposal. In 1749, the mission was reestablished along the north side of the San Antonio River and the presidio along the south, approximately one mile distant. The new emplacements were to care for the Piquicanes, Tamiques, Taranames and Manos de Perros Indians; these were scattered, indigenous tribes belonging to the Coahuiltecan, or Pakawa, group.

Also in 1749, the presidio at La Bahía installed a new commandant, Manuel Ramírez de la Piscina. Ramírez held the administration of the presidio for seventeen years until his death in 1767. During his tenure, as well as those who followed, La Bahía was besieged variously by Comanche and Lipan (Apache) natives. The presidio's small contingent of *escoltas* (armed soldiers) had much difficulty in preventing the usually nocturnal raids. Indeed, the region's protectors typically chased only stragglers of the attacks hours later; a successful counterattack occurred if the soldiers re-collected some of the horses, sheep or cattle that had been taken in the night.

Due to the Indians' internal conflicts (those to whom the Franciscans were ministering, the Tonkawa, Aranama and Tamique, were inimical to the Comanche and Apache; the Comanche to the Apache; and so on), Ramírez devised to construct another mission close enough to the de Loreto Presidio and Espíritu Santo Mission that the escoltas might be able to protect it yet distant enough that the religious could tend to the spiritual needs of the Karankawan tribes without hostilities flaring. The solution was Nuestra Señora del Rosario Mission, located about two leagues (less than five miles) from the existing two structures. These three, then, would be incorporated into the name La Bahía.

Father Juan de Dios María Cameros, from the college at Zacatecas, was placed in charge of the new mission in November 1754. Relatively distant from the other two buildings, Rosario never enjoyed the same spiritual success as its sister mission, those around San Antonio or even in El Paso. The Karankawa were interested in the religious's lessons when a food source

Façade of church at La Bahía Presidio. *Image courtesy of author.*

was available. More often than not, if not fed at the mission, these *indios bravos* would regress back into the woods and the coastal areas and revert to their pagan customs. As is evident from the records kept, in the first four years the number of baptisms at the new mission was still in the low double digits. However, while the Indians did not congregate at La Bahía in the numbers that the Franciscans desired, there was sufficient progress to sustain the missions in that region for several years.

From 1767 to 1768, Father Gaspar José de Solís, from the college at Zacatecas, made an inspection tour of many of the missions north of the Rio Grande del Norte. While visiting the mission of Nuestra Santísima de Rosario (another name for Rosario), Solís wrote in his diary:

> The church is very decent, of good wood and plastered with mud on the inside, trimmed and roofed with good beams (vigas) and shingled so that it is as a dome. Its adornment is very neat and clean. The sacred ornamental vessels are neat, the pulpit, confessional, and altar utensils and all things pertaining to the divine worshipper very good, in place, and in due form and order, as also is its baptismal font with its silver shell, the

hour glass of silver for the holy extreme Unction.... The minister of it who is...Fray Joseph Escovar, works much for its improvement, increase, and advancement. He conducts himself with the Indians with a great deal of love, charity, gentleness, and in a mild manner. He has them work, teaches them to pray, tries to catechise them by instructing them in civilization and the rudiments of the Holy Faith.

However, as regards the missionaries' charges, Solís was not as impressed:

They are all barbarous, lazy, weak, indolent, are also so fond of dainties and gluttonous that they eat meat almost raw, underdone, or parboiled, or half roasted and dripping blood. The men prefer to suffer naked and unsheltered, which they do not suffer when in the mission where the father assists them in everything, in eating, dressing, and other necessities, and in conveniences by being in the woods or on the beach at their liberty and giving themselves to leisure and all kinds of vices, especially to that of luxury, thieving, robbery, and dancing, which is common to all. They are very much given to the dances, which they call "mitotes" of which for some there are feasts and merry making and others are sad and mournful.... The Indian men in these dances seem like demons by the grimaces that they make.

Father Solís continues, unfortunately but honestly, about the customs of these tribes after they have made war against one another. He writes that the victims procured by the Indians are first tied to a stake in the ground and

Native American artifacts from Mission Rosario. *Courtesy of Texas Archaeological Research Laboratory.*

with knives well sharpened in their hands, dancing and leaping they approach the victim and cut a piece from his body. They go to the fire and half roast it, and in the vicinity of the sufferer they eat it with great relish and thus they go on tearing it to pieces and quartering it until they clear it of flesh and it dies. They do not cast the bones away, but divide them among each other and him that plays [the "music" of the mitote] *they go about sucking them until they almost consume them. They do the same with the religious and Spanish if they find any.*

Solís continues the bloody story, and it is as unpleasant as the previous quotation. When Father Solís had left Rosario, he made his way to the area's other mission and presidio. He entered the Mission Bahía del Espíritu Santo on March 6, 1768; by March 11, he had informed himself of the condition of all three structures. Of Espíritu Santo and de Loreto, Solís wrote:

This mission is better than the preceding one of Santísimo Rosario. It is situated on the banks of the San Antonio de Béxar River, which is full of running water as I have said and has pleasant banks and many fish. Near by the Royal presidio, which is no more than half the distance across the river which is crossed in a canoe, is the church which is smaller than that of Rosario, but large enough.[24]

Father Solís left the Goliad region in March 1768 and trekked west toward the virid fields of the San Antonio missions and presidio. He found them flourishing; indeed, those missions would become the standard whereby the other Texas missions were to be graded. However, within forty years the Rosario mission had recorded 200 baptisms. Considering the difficulty of the work, this figure appears impressive. Espíritu Santo, that same sacred rite, covering the same time period, accounted a figure of 620 baptisms and also achieved 278 Christian burials. Of these figures, though, there is always uncertainty. As Walter McCaleb noted, "Much of the data about the missions is [*sic*] uncertain in character. Take that about Rosario, where figures about baptisms, etc., are in utter conflict."[25] This writer, too, has found many similar discrepancies not only among the figures mentioned but also as concerns dates, number of personnel and which Mexican college was in charge of which missions.

In the end, all of the Spanish structures making up La Bahía began to deteriorate. Even though the region was enormously successful in creating

Interior/altar, Espíritu Santo/La Bahía. *Image courtesy of Angie Browne.*

large herds of cattle, many factors eventually resulted in the missions' decline. First and foremost was the reluctance of the native tribes to congregate at the missions and accept the instruction that the Franciscans offered. The idea of settling into such a confined area was a European model that the

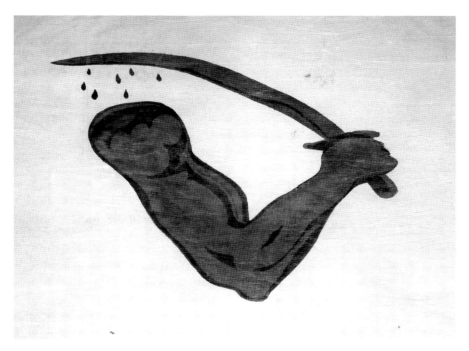

"Fort Defiance" flag. *Image courtesy of Angie Browne.*

Texas Indians often found alienating and absurd. Second, the administration of the missionaries' work was handled hundreds of miles away in Mexico by authorities who had no real understanding of the true situation in *la tierra adentro*. Decisions were made that often either had deleterious results or were simply short-sighted. Ultimately, though, it was the secularization of the missions that defeated them. After the government's decision to turn the land and buildings over to local populace and clergy (the secularization decree of April 10, 1794), the Franciscans found their authority usurped and their positions recalled back to their respective colleges. As Quirarte observed:

> *Following the expulsion of the Jesuits from the Americas by the king [Charles II], the missions in Pimeria Alta (the Mexican state of Sonora and southern Arizona) were turned over to the Franciscans from the college of the Holy Cross in Querétaro. This forced the Querétarans to pull back from the mission field in Texas in order to fulfill their new responsibilities. They therefore requested and were granted permission to*

leave their missions in Texas. In 1772 the missions were turned over to the Zacarecan missionaries, who administered them for the remainder of their stay in Texas.[26]

The missions fell into disrepair upon their departure. Indeed, the nineteenth century witnessed more and more Anglo immigration. This, coupled with the volatile political situation between Mexico and Spain in the same century, all but ensured the demise of the Franciscans' work. Mexico realized its independence from Spain in 1821, but the Franciscan friars continued to hold onto La Bahía until 1830, when Rosario, Espíritu Santo and the mission at Refugio, just about ten leagues south of Espíritu Santo, were formally secularized. As has happened the world over, when formal care is removed from an ancient site, the locals find better use for the structures' materials. Much of the stone, mortar and iron used at the missions and presidio were repurposed by residents to build homes, corrals and fences.

The presidio at Goliad, in 1836 mostly ruinous, save the church, was the site of Colonel James Fannin's surrender and infamous execution by Santa Anna's army. Renamed Fort Defiance by Fannin, he and over four hundred of his men surrendered to Mexico's General José de Urrea on March 20, nearly six weeks after taking defense at the presidio and two weeks after the fall of the "Alamo." Initially guaranteed safety, Fannin's men were marched out of the church on Palm Sunday, March 27, 1836, and summarily executed. Fannin was killed last, after having been made to witness the massacre of his men. Wounded and unable to stand, Fannin was shot, while seated, directly in front of the chapel's doors. At the La Bahía presidio can be seen a replica of the Texian flag from the period, depicting a red, defiant arm clutching a sanguinary sword. A rebellion that unfortunately ended with Fannin and his men's murders, along with the defeat at the Alamo, was the spur that drove many Texans to augment Sam Houston's army and ultimately gain victory at San Jacinto. The monument just southeast of the presidio marks the resting place of Fannin and his men's remains.

Over the next several decades, the presidio was also refuge for several other adventurers, who tried to use the remains of the old fort as protection and a resource for their own militaristic plots.

The church mentioned earlier is the chapel of the presidio. This chapel was almost all that remained of the presidio for several years and was the nucleus at which the reconstruction took place many years later. Its reconstruction was begun in the early twentieth century and continued well into the 1940s.

Reconstruction at La Bahía, 1930s. *Courtesy of Texas Parks and Wildlife Department.*

It is interesting to note that much of the stone (quarried from the riparian areas around the nearby river) used to replace the presidio's walls was removed from the ruinous Rosario mission. One need only visit the presidio to see that the amount of stone carried from one to the other must have been enormous. The wall around the presidio, approximately two thousand feet square, is patched with the mission's rock. When archaeologists complained that the stone's removal hindered their work at Rosario, the state unloaded thousands of pounds of replacement rock near the Rosario site, evidently considering that one rock is as good as another. This can still be seen—it is the rock alongside the road as one drives past the old mission. Presently, the county and state are deciding what to do with Rosario. The idea at the moment is to build an overview, a sort of scenic patio from which the public can view the site from a safe distance. Archaeological studies have been suspended for a time.

La Bahía Mission, in turn, was converted into, first, an all-women's college, and then another institution of higher learning, Aranama College. This school remained in use from 1852 until the beginning of the American Civil

Presidio at La Bahía, southeast view. *Image courtesy of author.*

Reconstruction at La Bahía, 1930s. *Courtesy of Texas Parks and Wildlife Department.*

War, when, as is written in various sources, the entire student body enlisted in the Confederate army. The structure stood for a while until damaged by a hurricane later in the century. A fire soon thereafter destroyed what was left of the friars' work. Care or maintenance of the building did not arrive until the early 1930s, when Goliad County decided to preserve the area as a state park. Next, from 1933 to 1941, the Civilian Conservation Corps (CCC), with the guidance of the University of Texas and the National Parks Service, began a complete reconstruction of the mission at its old site, restoring it to its earlier appearance as determined by historians and archaeologists.

As for the location of the original sites of the mission and presidio, near Gracitas Creek, where La Salle had begun his colony, archaeological efforts beginning in the 1960s and continuing through the early 1980s have found remains of both Spanish and French occupation. Perhaps it is fitting that evidence of both La Salle and Fray Massanet should be found within the same area, while that of the Native Americans, which both parties tried to embrace but for disparate reasons, is more often found outside those boundaries.

CHAPTER 3

THE MISSIONS AND PRESIDIOS OF EL PASO

The Franciscans' work in west Texas is commonly seen to have stemmed from the New Mexican Pueblo Revolt of 1680, when the rebel Indian El Popé ("Pó Pay") and his Tiguan confederates drove their conquerors east. The Spanish terminated their retreat at the Rio Grande, near today's El Paso. It was from here that Antonio de Otermín, the governor of the New Mexico territory, would stage the Spanish reconquest of New Mexico twelve years later. But the rebellion had demonstrated a most severe brutality and rage, the sort that can only arise from a long-suppressed anger and endured humility. From emotions this raw, no one can ever fully recover or be convinced of their wrongheadedness at lashing out. In some ways, the Puebloans of New Mexico, like some regions of Mexico proper, have never fully accepted their westernization; in some areas the old, traditional ways coexist with those of the Franciscans. And in some ways, the Spanish were to blame for their own injury.

From the conquest of Cortés forward, those indigenous tribes that the Spanish tried to subdue continually and repeatedly made efforts to reclaim their traditions. Once the submission was accomplished within the Mexican interior, the Indians worked with the Spanish soldiers in erecting missions, presidios and other structures for the colonial government. Often, the *indios* embedded icons of their former gods within the tiles and caliche that formed these new buildings so that they could worship the old with the new. In other instances, natives secreted their idols into their homes or caves and continued to worship surreptitiously, at times immediately after receiving catechism.

In the regions that would become Texas, the Indians were not naturally inclined to life within mission walls. They accepted the Franciscans' offerings only reluctantly and infrequently. In New Mexico, the pueblo was akin to the European town, but a singular dwelling space and farmed land were where the similarities ended. While the Indians in Louisiana and Texas ranged within and without the missions, now adhering to the religious's ideals and mandates, then returning to their woods and antique customs, the Indians of New Mexico remained stationary inside the pueblo, coursing only between home and mission. Succoring idols within the *estufas* was a more difficult practice to conceal when these temples were permanent fixtures of the community. Of course, the Franciscans allowed none of that and frequently punished those who continued to worship the old gods. At times these punishments were corporal and severe.

The Spanish, as stated earlier, had discovered these settlements in the sixteenth century. Cabeza de Vaca had wandered close enough that he was told about these cities. Coronado had a very real experience there while he vanquished and suppressed the indigenous populace, resulting, finally, in the bloody Tiguex War of 1540–41. Antonio de Espejo, with Father Beltrán, had traveled through New Mexico in 1582–83, ostensibly to seek out two Franciscans who had insisted on remaining in the region from an earlier expedition. However, Espejo's actual goal was to find land for his cattle enterprise. He had used the search-and-rescue theme as a way to garner official sanction for his entrada. The two religious, by the way, were found, both martyred by the native tribes to whom they ministered. Over a century later, Peñalosa had tried his hand at maintaining the New Mexican region, failing brilliantly enough to draw rebuke and indictment from the Inquisition. While Peñalosa had been the final straw, the Puebloans had suffered much more directly after Coronado. Juan de Oñate, the son of a wealthy silver mine owner and *encomendero*, would lead a fateful expedition near the end of the sixteenth century, illustrating for the New Mexican Indians just how the Spanish perceived them.

Juan de Oñate was a new breed of Spaniard. He was born in the New World at Zacatecas. Early on, he was involved in conquering those lands just below the Rio Grande. He married Isabel de Tolosa Cortés Moctezuma, a descendant of both the conquistador and the Aztec ruler. Certainly his view of this region was markedly different from those who had traveled there before. His early adulthood was spent subduing the Indians of northern Mexico, prospecting for silver mines and assisting

Interior of Ysleta Mission, circa 1860. *University of Texas at El Paso Library Special Collections Department, Cleofas Calleros Papers.*

the religious in establishing missions. As such, Oñate would surely have seen the area and its resources as his birthright.

In September 1595, King Philip II of Spain awarded Oñate a contract to settle and colonize the territory of Santa Fé de Nuevo México, a tract of land extending from north central Mexico through present-day New Mexico and stretching across west Texas. It was believed back in Madrid that this region contained wealth on a scale matching what Cortés had discovered. The crown hoped that this settlement would help heal the injury inflicted by the English in the defeat of the Spanish Armada in 1588. Accordingly, this entrada was expected to be immense. Since the expedition's leader was to cover much of the cost himself, Oñate, with his famously rich father, was elected to oversee the enterprise.

The expedition left Mexico in January 1598 with 400 soldiers (130 had families who accompanied the entrada), several hundred Mexican Indians and thousands of heads of stock. They marched up the Rio Conchos, with the river on their right, and then, historically, Oñate veered left through the dunes of Chihuahua to a new pass over the Rio Grande, one he named El Paso del Río del Norte. The company reached the river in April and had crossed by early May, with Oñate claiming all the lands north of the river for Spain. By July, Oñate had traveled well into the area and established the first European settlement within New

Mexico, an old pueblo site called Ohkay Owingeh, now renamed San Juan de los Caballeros.

The stated purpose of this expedition was to spread Roman Catholicism among the indigenous tribes. To that end, ten Franciscans joined the group, and missions were constructed, including one at San Juan. However, many in Oñate's group fully expected the same riches that the Spanish government was hoping for. They were to be disappointed. The land was nowhere near as fecund as that in central Mexico, and the natives proved just as hostile. When the wealth did not materialize quickly, many in the expedition grew surly, some dissented and others deserted. However, no matter the quarrel, the result, according to most historians, was the same: Oñate ruled with an iron fist.

The next year, Oñate moved his capital seat farther north to San Gabriel de Yunque-Ouinge. This colony, just as San Juan, comprised a military garrison, new houses and a church. From here, Oñate divided his soldiers into smaller contingents, and these simultaneously explored the territories east and west of San Gabriel. Oñate, as the area's first European governor, was required to establish *encomiendas* throughout this new province. This he did while exploring the region, telling all of the respective pueblo chiefs, through translators, that they now were Spanish subjects and owed annual tribute. The Franciscans knew already that such heavy-handed tactics would not rest well with the indigenous populace; they knew that if any pueblo was unable to pay with money or goods, the Spanish would translate that tribute to forced labor. The religious opted instead for a more equal taxation policy, that of *décimo*, whereby Spanish settler and native alike paid only one-tenth of their harvest for the succor of the missions and regional churches. But the new governor had his orders and proceeded as before. This feudal system, coupled with what by now were regular abuses, was to have dire consequences for the new colonies and Oñate.

Upon settling at San Gabriel, Oñate appointed his nephew Juan de Zaldívar as *maestre de campo*. Zaldívar, in December 1598, would lead a small contingent of soldiers on one of Oñate's several scouting expeditions, one that would take the team to the pueblo of Acoma, the "Sky City." That same year, the Acoma chief, Zutacapan, understood that the Spanish were coming to overthrow him and his pueblo and take their food, resources and customs by force, just as Coronado had tried earlier. This time, the Indians decided to resist.

Arriving at Acoma, a small group of sixteen soldiers, including the young Zaldívar, climbed the 360-odd feet to the top of the mesa to ask for some

Socorro Mission, nineteenth century. *University of Texas at El Paso Library Special Collections Department, Tom Lea Papers.*

food while the main body of soldiers waited below with the supplies and horses. What occurred next is variously reported. In some accounts, the Indians flatly refused to assist, and this enflamed the Spanish. Other reports state that, while waiting, the soldiers acted on their licentious thoughts. Still another story is that Zutacapan was simply waiting to ambush them. In any event, Zaldívar and ten of his men were ambushed and killed by the Acoma Indians; those soldiers waiting below became aware of the situation when they first heard gunshots and then saw a couple of their comrades' bodies falling toward them from the mesa above. A moment later, these same soldiers witnessed more of their friends leaping from the mesa as their only way to safety, some landing in such a way that they only sustained broken bones; others were broken to bits. The survivors retreated back to Oñate.

When the governor heard this news, he was enraged. Not only were eleven of his men dead, but one of them was his nephew. Oñate ordered Zaldívar's brother Vicente de Zaldívar to lead the force against Acoma Pueblo. Vicente, with seventy men and cannons, went in pursuit of revenge.

Zaldívar arrived at Acoma on January 21, 1599. Reports indicate that the fighting was back and forth for two full days, the Spanish arquebus being less effective due to the natural defenses. However, on the third day, Zaldívar brought up the small cannons and proceeded to blast his way onto the mesa. Once breached, the pueblo was overrun. The Indians' main defense had been the terrain; with that advantage lost, the Massacre of Acoma began. The Spanish cannons not only ripped through flesh, but they also tore through the buildings, igniting walls and roofs as the shots roared by. Soon, much of the mesa was ablaze. Of the two thousand warriors, five hundred were killed. In addition, the Spanish killed approximately three hundred women and children and took another five hundred as slaves. However, even this did not diminish Oñate's bloodlust. He ordered that all males above twenty-five years old should have their right feet amputated and that males between twelve and twenty-five were to be enslaved and serve terms of twenty years, presumably in the silver mines of Coahuila. Many of the women and children were doled out to families, churches and convents in Mexico as slaves. In the end, only twenty-four young men were made to suffer these atrocities. It should be noted that as recently as January 1998, when New Mexico was to celebrate the 400th anniversary of the first Spanish settlements there, a twelve-foot bronze statue of Oñate was dedicated at Española, New Mexico. Early one morning, workers noticed that the right foot—boot, stirrup and spur—had been sawn off. The Indians of Acoma Pueblo took credit for the destruction, or, as they viewed the act, retribution.[27]

When news of the massacre reached King Philip, he was horrified. Oñate was severely reprimanded soon afterward and exiled from New Mexico forever and from Mexico for a period of four years. He was also to report to Spain to answer the charges against him. However, in 1607, he resigned his post as governor before the news from Madrid reached him. Oñate was evidently tired of the Spanish citizens' complaints and financial trouble. He did eventually return to Spain, dying there a quarter of a century later. With his exit, New Mexico breathed a sigh of relief. For the next several decades, Spanish, Franciscan and Indian enjoyed a relative calm. But the storm had only retreated; it had not dissipated.

During the next eight decades, the Franciscans tried their best to develop beneficial relationships with the Indians of New Mexico. However, the relationships forged between the Spanish colonists and the natives was a much different story. The encomienda system maintained that the province's governor could, as he saw fit, grant title and land to certain Spaniards (those who had held possession of their land for a minimum of five years; for many, a period too long to maintain). This grant not only offered land, tribute and resources to the holder; it also obligated him to lend assistance, both material and martial, to the Franciscans within his area. Because these *encomenderos* often found much use for the labor and resources of the indigenous populace, the religious frequently found themselves acting as mediators between the Spanish colonists and their neophyte charges when the latter had grievances.

The interval between Oñate's tenure and the Pueblo Revolt of 1680 was relatively inactive, although only from the placid perspective of distance. Because most of the Spanish records from the interval of 1600–80 were lost or destroyed due to the magnitude of the revolt, little documentation exists for us. However, what does remain is remarkable, including the "Memorial" of Father Alonso de Benavides, the *custos*, or guardian, of the Franciscans in New Mexico from 1626 to 1629. This document is rich with information concerning those intervening years from Oñate to El Popé. The account includes reference to the many pueblo Indian tribes and the Franciscans' efforts to convert them. Additionally, Benavides's writing includes clear descriptions of New Mexico's geology, wildlife and even an acknowledgement of the presence of María de Jesús de Agreda among the Xumanas (Jumanos) Indians. Indeed, Benavides was so enthralled by the Jumanos' stories about the apparitional appearance of the "Lady in Blue" that, upon his return to Spain, Benavides sought out Sister Agreda to confirm what the natives had related to him. But Benavides had not always found such agreeable natives during his journey into New Mexico.

Father Benavides had traveled to New Mexico along the Camino Real, that rugged path now worn smooth by earlier explorers like Espejo and Oñate, stretching from Mexico City to Santa Fe. Of his encounter with those tribes he met closer to El Paso del Norte, Benavides wrote: "We have tried all possible [means] to convert and pacify these nations as well for

Façade of Ysleta Mission, circa 1890. *University of Texas at El Paso Library Special Collections Department, Cleofas Calleros Papers.*

the good of their souls as for the security of the road. But so great is their barbarism that they will not even let themselves be talked with."[28] However, a stagnant attitude would not deter one such as Benavides. He was, literally, a man on a mission, and his thoughts reached far beyond first impressions. Ever the diplomat, Benavides was also acutely aware of the politics that the Franciscans had to deal with in order to accrue the resources they needed to continue the effort of saving souls. By now, in the short history of the religious's trials in trying to temper both the indigenous tribes and those of the soldiers and colonists, it had become clear that the Franciscans needed to persuade both bureaucrat and "barbarian" alike if they were to succeed. Massanet, Hidalgo and Margil had understood the importance of politics to their respective operations. Benavides was clear in his report that he knew what Madrid needed to hear. When writing of the New Mexican territory, Benavides reported:

> *This* [land] *is full of very great treasures of mines, very rich and prosperous in silver and gold....In particular, the hill of the pueblo of Socorro, chief* [town] *and head of this Province of the Piros. For all of it is of very prosperous minerals, which run from north to south more than fifty leagues; and for want of someone who might understand it and spend* [money] *on working it, the greatest riches in the world are not enjoyed, and your Majesty loses your Royal fifths.*[29]

Keenly aware that these remarks would garner royal attention, Benavides does his best to tie the goals of his mission with those of the Spanish government. Even though the spiritual health of the Indians is what the religious primarily sought, Father Benavides is not so smug or naive as to pretend that he is unaware of the reality. He writes that the Indians could be used as labor, if only the mines "were administered by persons of moderate greed, who would treat the Indians well and pay them for their work." For the Franciscan, living and working side by side would breech whatever social chasms might separate Spanish from Indian.

Later, with the skill of an ancient Roman orator, Benavides tactfully combines the prospects of both the church and government. Cognizant of the fact that persuasion rolls forward most easily on wheels greased with flattery, he concludes the appeal portion of his letter by declaring:

> *Though here it is clearly and evidently seen that God is the author and prime mover, for which we give Him infinite thanks. We owe them also*

Altar of Ysleta Mission, early twentieth century. *University of Texas at El Paso Library Special Collections Department, Cleofas Calleros Papers.*

> *to your Majesty, since without your Royal aid we could not have borne so many expenses. And your Majesty should be very proud to be the cause of all this change; who enjoy all the merit of those conversions, wherein we snatch so many thousands of souls from the claws of the Demon, a thing that could not be, save by a miracle.*[30]

The boldness and diplomacy of Benavides guaranteed that the king would continue to sponsor the brothers' work; several new missions were established in New Mexico in the next few years.

As customary, it was Benavides's task to inspect these missions and parish churches. While visiting settlements to the south (following the course of the Rio Grande), the custos was made aware of the Apache tribes, a nation so large that "it spreads out in places so much that we have not found an end to it."[31] Intent on locating some terminus for these people, Benavides turned east, toward Texas, and soon was met by a delegation of the Jumanos. These Indians greeted the religious with a rudimentary but seemingly prescient knowledge of the Catholic faith and even a few crudely made icons. These Indians claimed that they had, for a few years, been regularly visited by a "Woman in Blue" who instructed them in the ways of Christianity and had even told them to head west in search of more corporal beings who could give further instruction in the faith. When Benavides questioned them:

> *They* [the Xumanas] *replied that a woman like that one whom we had painted—which was a picture of the Mother Luisa de Carron—used to preach to each one of them in their* [our] *tongue, telling them that they should come to summon the Fathers to instruct and baptize them, and that they should not be slothful* [about it]. *And that the woman who preached to them was dressed precisely like her who was painted there; but that the face was not like that one, but that she* [their visitant] *was young and beautiful. And always whenever Indians came newly from these nations, looking upon the picture and comparing it among themselves, they said that the clothing was the same but the face* [was] *not because the* [face] *of the woman who preached to them was* [that] *of a young and beautiful girl.*[32]

Benavides recognized the blue habit. It was the same as that worn by the nuns belonging to the Order of the Immaculate Conception, or the *Conceptionists* in Spain. The Indians gathered among the religious in droves. Benavides writes that when Fray Salas asked the congregation, standing outside in a wide field, who wished to receive the holy sacrament of baptism, not only did every native raise their arm, but even the mothers holding infants took them by their little arms and held them upward. While it is, of course, part of the genre of history writing to exaggerate numbers (see Herodotus's writing of the Persians' million-man army), Benavides does write that at this solemn occasion there were "more than ten thousand souls." His claim that all the gathered natives eagerly participated in the ceremony is difficult to dispute. After all, this tribe did seek out the religious, rather than the other way around. But while the Jumanos were willing converts, the Puebloans were formulating a much different opinion of their new neighbors—it was an opinion founded on observation of the interaction between the Franciscans and the rest of the Spanish colonists.

The governance of New Mexico was not a particularly enticing occupation. After Oñate's term, twenty-five others held the position of governor in the region, spanning the years 1607–80, with only a few managing the post for a term of more than five years; most held a tenuous hold for only one or two years. However, what most of the governors had in common was

Interior of Ysleta Mission, mid-nineteenth century. *University of Texas at El Paso Library Special Collections Department.*

a willingness to abuse their power and anger the Franciscans. Several and varied are the stories of these politicians leading expeditions for the sole purpose of capturing slave labor, indulging prurient motivations with the native women or exercising excessive and even lethal punishments for the recalcitrant. The encomienda system became harsh and abusive. The land in New Mexico did not yield the wealth the original colonists had hoped for, and this made them resentful. That anger flashed in every direction. To make up for their perceived loss of capital, these encomenderos frequently enrolled the natives to work, farming a near anemic landscape to supply the colonists with sustenance, weaving blankets or tanning hides for the settlers' profit. All this was in addition to the annual tribute already owed. New governors were reluctant to accept their appointments, knowing the hostile and difficult atmosphere that awaited them. As such, their administrations were marked by obsequiousness toward the colonists and cruelty toward the Puebloans. In turn, the religious often watched horrified as their neophyte charges were driven to desperation through neglect, enslavement and punishments. The Franciscans argued with the administration over the abuses and tried to reason with the colonists—all with little effect. In response, the missionaries resorted to the only tools at their disposal: the pen and the king. The friars wrote several letters detailing the deteriorating situation in the area, but as has been noted, news traveled very slowly. In frustration, the fathers tried to withhold the sacraments from colonists and politicians alike, but this only fueled the resident anger. As a last resort, the Franciscans excommunicated some and even succeeded in bringing others before the dreaded Inquisition. However, again, their letters of protest did not move as quickly as the pens that wrote them. This situation, as obscene as it was, could not sustain itself for long; indeed, it is surprising that it lasted for as many years as it did.

The exploitation only increased with the passing years. Settler and governor alike helped themselves to whatever resource was available. This, in combination with Apache attacks and acquired European diseases, did little to help the Franciscans' goals. Further, the encomenderos routinely established *rancherias* (cattle and sheep ranches) on land designated by the crown for the Puebloans' farmland. Insult to injury was the drought that began around 1670, an event that the Puebloan medicine men blamed on the Christians. And, all the while, the Puebloans watched as their new spiritual leaders, the Franciscans, feuded with their own kind. It should come as no surprise that the Indians reacted violently to this situation. The only surprise is that their response took several decades to develop; one could make the assumption that the friars' tenacious determination to instill peace in every portion of their communities was one cause for the natives' Hamlet-like hesitancy.

In addition to the Puebloans' anger due to their subjugation, their consternation toward the Franciscans was augmented when the latter consistently refused to allow the natives to continue their religious practices. While fully aware that the ancient Romans were successful in their expansion efforts mainly by allowing the conquered to retain their heritage, religion and, oftentimes, their royalty and governments, the Spanish, and in particular the Franciscans, were intractable when it came to allowing the natives the right to ancient ritual. Indeed, Father Alonso de Posada, while working at a New Mexican mission in the 1670s, forbade every dance in relation to Kachina (the Puebloan spirits for nearly every aspect of their lives) and ordered all Kachina masks, dolls, icons and other paraphernalia to be taken up and burned. In addition, the kivas, or the centers for this worship, were also to be destroyed. The drugs taken by the shamans to facilitate their spiritual journeys were banned. Over time, the fire of the natives' resentment toward the religious burned as hot as that toward Spanish encomenderos, soldiers and government officials. Mutual malice increased over the years until the missionaries' anger obliged them to inflict very strict punishments on those who ignored the new religion in favor of the antique one. Obviously, the strain of all this hostility tearing in every direction would eventually rend the entire situation to pieces. And in 1680, that is exactly what occurred.

Juan Francisco Treviño was chosen as governor of the New Mexico territory in 1675. By many accounts, his primary job was to try and eradicate the religious heritage of the native Indians. To that end, Treviño ordered the destruction of the aforementioned icons, temples and traditions. In a separate but conjoined effort, Treviño also arrested forty-seven shamans for executing the murder of a few Spanish religious and perpetuating pagan rituals. Of these, four were sentenced to the gallows. Three from the group were summarily hanged, and the fourth committed suicide before his turn. The other forty-three were scourged and imprisoned. The outrage at this enticed nearly one hundred warriors to surround Treviño's headquarters at the governor's palace in Santa Fe and demand the release of the prisoners. Because many of the Spanish soldiers were away fighting Apache tribes, few were on hand to defend the governor's residence. The palace was stormed, and Treviño was taken prisoner. He was only allowed to ransom himself by the release of the medicine men. Among these was a certain shaman of the Tewa pueblo, Po'Pay, known more commonly as Popé.

Popé, having retreated to Taos, began the task of usurping Spanish rule in New Mexico. Although the region's tribes had been at times inimical toward one another, Popé now was successful in uniting them against a common enemy. His plan was simple enough: rid the region of the Spanish, destroy the missions and churches of the Franciscans and restore the old religious traditions. To this end, Popé called upon the leaders of the pueblos for allegiance. Most agreed eagerly.

The method employed by Popé to mask the day of revenge is almost as famous a tale as Alexander's Gordian knot. Popé delivered to each confederate pueblo a piece of rope with several knots tied along its length. The leaders of each pueblo were to untie one knot each day until the last, that being the day of conspiracy, August 13, 1680. This technique was sure to keep the Spanish unaware of the plot. Indeed, the plan worked very well and was even facilitated when Popé murdered his own son-in-law, whom he feared might betray the plot to the Spanish.

Although the Spanish were eventually made aware of the plan from the capture of a couple of Indian messengers, the plot was only revealed a couple of days before the revolt. As a result, word was broadcast to begin earlier, on August 10. The governor, Antonio de Otermín, became aware of the sprung trap when word of a priest's martyrdom (Father Juan Pio) was delivered on that day. Panic soon followed the news, and many Spaniards escaped into Mexico; others retreated to the governor's residence at Santa Fe. By August 15, an estimated one thousand Spanish were holed up at the

Interior of San Elizario Presidio. *Image courtesy of Angie Browne.*

governor's palace, with well over twice that number of Indians besieging the area. Many other Spanish took refuge in the pueblo at Isleta, home to an Indian group that had not taken part in the conspiracy.

From the beginning of the revolt, Otermín had tried to resist and even counterattacked on a number of occasions. However, after a few days' fighting, the governor had to abandon the situation when he realized that the Indians were being reinforced while he was not. By August 21, the Spanish at Santa Fe (estimated at nearly two thousand, a number that included a few hundred Indians) began their arduous trek south toward El Paso del Norte. Popé followed, but he allowed the retreat simply because the Spanish were obviously leaving the territory. Otermín intercepted those Spanish settlers also retreating south from Isleta on September 3. Together, they continued the retreat southward. Stopping at intervals for "councils of war," Otermín was determined, for some weeks, to find a way to retake New Mexico. Finally, convinced by the colonists and religious that further counterattacks were futile, Otermín agreed to continue all the way to Rio del Paso and created a provisional settlement there from which to stage the Spanish reoccupation. Upon arrival, and meeting up with a supply train from Mexico, Otermín began the job of establishing the colony of Pueblo del Paso. To this end, he commissioned the construction of missions in the area for the colonists and the Indians who had accompanied them. This new settlement, named San Lorenzo, was located just southeast of present-day El Paso.

Tempting as it is, it would be a mistake to assume that these refugees were the first settlers in the El Paso region. The area just south of present-day El Paso had been settled, if only partially, by the Spanish for a number of years before Otermín and his train limped into the region. One governor of Nueva Vizcaya, Francisco de Gorraez Beaumont, had, some years before the revolt, sent a correspondence informing one of his officers to help establish the territories northward toward the Rio Grande. As Anne Hughes notes:

> *In the second year of his rule, 1663, in response to the call of the Indians around Casas Grandes* [an ancient and abandoned Indian site that is, today, a UNESCO site in the northern portion of the state of Chihuahua] *for missionaries, Governor Beaumont ordered Captain Andres Garcia, who was settling on the Rio del Norte, "confines of La Vizcaya in New Mexico," to pass to Casas Grandes, with his family and certain others of his kindred who might assist him; Captian Garcia was further ordered to promote the settlement of Casa Grandes and to endeavor to congregate the largest number of Indians possible.*[33]

In this now more heavily occupied region, yet another Indian revolt occurred in 1684. Led by a confederacy of Mansos, Apaches, Janos and a few other tribes, these Spanish colonists, along with the few Indians of the Piros and Tigua tribes who had stayed faithful to the Spanish, consolidated themselves near the great bend in the river and nearer the established mission of Nuestra Señora de Guadlalupe. Amid persistent Indian attacks and crop failures, these Spanish colonists had asked permission to abandon the area, but they were rebuffed by the provincial government in Mexico. Ultimately, it was this decision that solidified the El Paso settlement. The next governor, Don Domingo Jironza Petriz de Cruzate, took over for Otermín in 1683; obviously, it was he who had to contend with the revolt of 1684 and the many complaints, territorial disputes and decisions about when and how to retake the New Mexico region.

The revolt of 1680 had left over four hundred Spanish dead, including women and children, along with twenty-one of the thirty-three priests in the region. The missions and churches were burned, and all things known to be sacred to the Franciscans were desecrated and destroyed. The homes of the colonists and most other Spanish buildings were also burned. Popé declared a new state in which he was the supreme ruler; all were to revert to the old, traditional lifestyles. As stated by a native, one Pedro Naranjo of the Queres Nation, under interrogation in December 1681, Popé's immediate attentions were to be rid of all things Spanish: "He [Popé] saw to it that they at once erected and rebuilt their houses of idolatry which they call estufas, and made very ugly masks in imitation of the devil in order to dance the dance of the cacina."[34]

Unfortunately, the drought that had begun several years earlier did not abate, and many of Popé's disciples began to doubt his spiritual talents. Several of the Puebloans began to take issue with Popé's aggressiveness and despotism; it was not long before infighting began anew. Likewise, the Apache and Navajo tribes, aware of the Spanish absence, raided the pueblos with renewed fervor. Twelve years later, the Spanish did reoccupy the region, led by then governor Don Diego de Vargas.

At a council held in Santa Fe in September 1692, Vargas wisely pardoned the native tribes that had participated in the revolt. This instance of prudence, coupled with the death of Popé in 1688, allowed the Spanish and the New Mexican Indians to settle into a relative calm for the next several decades. Vargas was, however, an exceedingly intolerant governor. During an absence from Santa Fe in 1693, the Indians again attempted a revolt. When Vargas returned, the punishments imposed were swift and severe.

Vargas had seventy natives executed and sentenced another four hundred to ten years' imprisonment, which often meant being handed over to Spanish families and government officials in Mexico in servitude.

Why so many had obsequiously gone where Popé directed is understood mainly by two factors. First was the ill treatment of the Indians by the Spanish. Colonists, governors and Franciscans alike had tried to subjugate the New Mexican Indians through force of will and violence. Second, the Puebloans greatly feared and respected their own religious, the shamans. It must be imagined to have been very difficult to abandon centuries of religious practice simply because one is told to do so. That many hundreds did is a testament to the Franciscans' determined efforts. Nevertheless, after the arrest of the forty-seven medicine men, Popé's stature rose exponentially with his injuries. He, along with a few others of the same group, came to be feared and revered more than before. One pueblo Indian described, nearly a year and a half after the revolt and under interrogation by Spanish authorities, why he and his countrymen had followed this home-styled messiah:

Mission Socorro. *Image courtesy of author.*

Ysleta Mission, early twentieth century. *University of Texas at El Paso Library Special Collections Department, Cleofas Calleros Papers.*

Asked why they held the said Popé in such fear and obeyed him, and whether he was the chief man of the pueblo, or a good Christian, or a sorcerer, he said that the common report that circulated and still is current among all the natives is that the said Indian Popé talks with the devil, and for this reason all held him in terror, obeying his commands although they were contrary to the orders of the senior governors, the prelate and the religious, and the Spaniards, he giving them to understand that the word which he spoke was better than that of all the rest.[35]

With the exception of a couple of attempts to retake New Mexico (one in 1681 and another six years later), the Spanish did not regain the region for twelve years. However, the intervening years did solidify the settlement at El Paso del Norte, since it was near there that Otermín first established a base camp from which the Spanish resolved to retake the New Mexican territory.

Many of the Tigua Indians (approximately 320) accompanied the Spanish in their retreat from New Mexico. The region designated for them in the El Paso area was named Ysleta del Sur ("Isleta of the South"). As mentioned earlier, the Spanish, once finding quietude from the revolt, set about the founding of new missions for both the colonists' and the natives' continued instruction in the Catholic faith. The first of these was named Corpus Christi de la Isleta. This mission was established in 1682 under the supervision of Otermín. Fray Francisco de Ayeta, from the college of Zacatecas, was given its charge. It was the first mission established within the borders of Texas. Initially, the mission was located on the south side of the Rio Grande, but subsequent flooding changed the riparian landscape, and the mission endured several location changes, at times requiring the mission to be rebuilt. At other times, most notably in the early nineteenth century, after the Rio Grande had eased its distended reach, the mission was to be found "over there," on the north bank. There was even a brief period, in the early eighteenth century, when all three structures were to be found along an island created by the river's raging.

Once Isleta was permanently connected to the area, the region acquired the presidio of San Elizario and another mission, Socorro, both established along the north bank of the Rio Grande. (It should be noted that Mission Nuestra Señora de Guadalupe was erected on the south side of the river, in Juarez, Mexico, in 1659, and it still stands today. Some claim that, due to the ever-changing course of the Rio Grande, this mission is, technically, the first Texas mission.)

Mission Corpus Christi de la Isleta is known to the people of El Paso and Juarez primarily because of its famous, shimmering dome. Known variously through the years as San Antonio de los Tiguas (the mission's original name, given by the Tigua Indians who had retreated to the area with the Spanish), San Lorenzo del Realito and Nuestra Señora del Monte Carmelo (the name given the mission in 1881 when the Jesuits gained possession), this mission has served the west Texas and northern Mexican community for well over three hundred years. However, the mission has endured as many changes in name as it has in structure. Indeed, the missions's reconstructions, relocations and restorations are its primary areas of interest from a historical point of view.

The mission today is undergoing extensive reconstruction and, as of the spring of 2016, is closed. Much of what is known of the earlier incarnations of the building was gleaned by archaeologists studying old records and the foundation. In fact, as James Burke writes:

> *Little remains of the original church. On May 15, 1907 its existing buildings were destroyed by fire. It had an oddly shaped hipped gable and a tower of three stages with a double belfry and an egg-shaped dome. It was ornamental and its style was probably a blend of Moorish and Romanesque. From the remains of the foundations we know that the church was 145 feet long and 18 feet wide, with a transept that measured 30 feet. It was constructed of masonry made of river-bed rock, gravel, and mortar, and it was composed of "unusual amounts of wooden supplements."*[36]

During a visit to the church in February 2016, the mission and its grounds were a hive of construction activity. A debris truck, like a distended cell, protruded from the front door. Workmen, like drones, methodically scaled the old roof while others could be heard hammering away inside the nave. When asked, several dates were given for completion of the reconstruction: one person said that the goal was May 2016; another said it was the autumn of the same year; and another stated that the work was so extensive that he thought the church might not be open for services until sometime in early 2017. Nevertheless, it was noted by this writer that many tourists, several from out of state, visit El Paso with the distinct goal of viewing the missions and presidio. As with most things, the date of the mission's reopening will most likely fall somewhere between the two extremes mentioned above. The people of El Paso and the Tigua Indians, on whose land all three missions rest, are eager to have the mission open and offering Mass again. That famous (or infamous, depending on your point of view) Spanish maxim of *mañana* (tomorrow) does not hold as much water here as in Spain. Here, there is an urgent sense of purpose among those concerned.

The missions and presidio of El Paso had a difficult birth and an even more arduous childhood. Born from fright and resistance, the fact that these structures have endured is a testament to the Franciscans' faith that their

Ysleta Mission under construction, 2016. *Image courtesy of author.*

work could produce a lasting lineage. The train of refugees, both Indian and Spaniard, from New Mexico was gradually deposited along the banks of the Rio Grande at various points: El Paso del Norte (Juarez), Senecu and Ysleta del Sur. Finally, five leagues farther southeast, the settlement of Socorro (like Ysleta, Socorro was also the name of a pueblo in New Mexico) was planted, and the Piro Indians were given this land. The mission of Nuestra Señora de la Limpia Concepcion del Socorro was founded, and Fray Antonio Guerra proffered the first Mass.

The mission at Socorro endured as many trials of faith as did that at Isleta. In 1683, only one year after its founding, some of the natives again conspired to revolt. This time the plot was to martyr Father Guerra and murder some of the Spanish families living at Socorro. Evidently, the plan was uncovered by some of the Zuma tribe, and the Spanish drove off to Isleta those conspirators they could identify. The others fled back to New Mexico, where anti-Spanish sentiment still prevailed. However, even with this violence ended, those settlements of the El Paso region still faced many hardships.

In 1692, due to the reoccupation of the New Mexican territory by Vargas, many Spaniards, along with some of the Piro, decided to return to their former homes there, reducing the Socorro population by almost half. That the Spanish authorities had, at the early stages of settling the El Paso region, segregated the several settlements between Spanish and Indian did little to kindle the latter's inclination toward the former. (At least eight, probably nine of these hamlets were founded, four for the Spanish, the remainder for the Indians.) Possibly in an effort to quell future resentment and violence, Father Joaquin de Hinojosa asked for and, somewhat surprisingly, received a land grant by the king of Spain, Charles III (or Carlos III). The grant, the largest in Texas's colonial period, comprised 177,136 acres of land. This enormous tract encompassed the territories of El Paso, Socorro, Isleta and Senecú. Additionally, Hinojosa was given not only ecclesiastical control of the area but also power as a private citizen. All of this had been agreed to by Governor Vargas, who was evidently willing to hand over some responsibility in the area while he focused on the reconquest of New Mexico.

The next several decades witnessed the halting growth of the Socorro area. Notwithstanding the early and frequent Indian uprisings, the village began

Altar at Socorro. *Image courtesy of author.*

to prosper, and official reports from the eighteenth and early nineteenth centuries give indication of a population of a few hundred—Spanish and Indian alike. Conversely, proximity to the Rio Grande was, again, to have a hand in the mission's future.

Those towns along the river below El Paso became Mexican settlements after the Mexican War of Independence in 1821. Less than eight years later, in the spring of 1829, the Rio Grande yet again deluged the region; the mission, churches and homes of Socorro were literally washed away. By the mid-nineteenth century, a third incarnation of the mission had been built. As reported by Professor Rex Gerald in an article from 1984:

> The congregation and mission occupied at least one previous locality in the El Paso del Norte area before moving to the present community area in the spring of 1684. The church and convent occupied several different sites within the area before the south-facing nave of the present church was completed in 1842–3. With the addition of the transept and sanctuary in 1876 the church proper was brought to its present configuration.[37]

The Jesuits, arriving in the area in 1881 after the "Expulsion of the Jesuits" during the Bourbon Reforms in Europe, were given charge of the mission. This group renamed Ysleta, calling it Nuestra Señora del Monte Carmelo, and took control of maintaining the now two-hundred-year-old missions in the area. During their administration, many repairs and restorations were undertaken, although one of their efforts nearly revived the riotous attitudes of the native populace.

Over three hundred years ago, an icon of St. Michael was literally carried (in an ox-drawn cart) to Socorro from Mexico and given its own special place near the altar. When, in the early twentieth century, the Jesuits wanted to reconstruct the ceiling and other interior portions of the mission, their plan was to remove the statue during construction. The locals did not approve. The image of St. Michael had come to mean much more to them than simply another icon; for the residents of Socorro, the statue was the embodiment of the mission and its faith-filled purpose. On the day the statue was to be taken and relocated to a Jesuit college in Mexico, the people of Socorro met the workmen at the front door, rifles loaded with buckshot and indignation. The icon was replaced and has held that position ever since.

By the latter part of the twentieth century, the mission was in desperate need of repair. In a newspaper article from the *El Paso Times* dated October 22, 1978, a reporter wrote, "The mission was rebuilt in 1840 after floods

St. Michael icon at Socorro. *Image courtesy of author.*

destroyed the original church. The seventeenth century construction methods and some of the original material, including the *vigas* (carved, wooden roof beams), were used in the new church."[38] Accordingly, from a report given by Professor Gerald in 1986, evidence is offered that the reconstruction workers tried to use what they could of the original building:

> *It seems entirely possible that the pre-1829 church was located adjacent to the rectory on the north and that the cemetery relocated earlier this century [twentieth] from that area was originally inside of and in the front of that church. The mound of fallen adobe that was the ruin of that flood-destroyed structure was probably utilized in the construction of the present church.*[39]

Socorro Mission today is a beautiful edifice. Referred to today simply as La Purisma, the gleaming white façade has been molded to resemble the ancient pueblo image of a thunderhead cloud, although some, maybe more orthodoxly minded, could envision a cruciform structure. In either case, the church absolutely radiates as one approaches. Evidently, many others have taken notice. The Socorro Mission was entered into the National Register of Historical Places in 1972.

The interior is still marvelous. The icon of St. Michael still stands on the far wall, on the right-hand side of the altar when facing the front door. The old, hand-carved and decorated vigas can still be clearly seen in the ceiling, still supporting the Franciscans' work after more than three centuries. The tiny room just to the right after entering is where the church has a small bookstore and information desk addressing the church's history. A recent visit found Magda Madureira Trujillo, a docent with the mission (she insists that she is simply a volunteer), offering some tourists a great deal of information about the mission's history. She explained, illustrated, directed and informed without ever needing to pause for thought. It was quite an amazing thing to witness someone so knowledgeable offering her time and energy so selflessly. When this writer finally caught her between visitors, she explained that her interest in the mission is inherent. She is, on her mother's side, Piro Indian and a resident of Socorro. She told of how she and others have, for many years now, been trying to broadcast information about the area's rich heritage. "We tend to catch fourth and fifth graders, because that's when they teach Texas history," she said when asked about the most regular visitors. Ms. Madureira also mentioned that Pope Francis's recent visit to Mexico in general and Juarez in particular "stimulated a lot of traffic!"

Standing outside, Ms. Madureira indicated a viga just inside the front door that has, in Spanish, the date of its re-installation (1821). After instinctively replacing her hat to fend off the Texas sun, she silently surveyed the entire grounds and the vast reach of land beyond. She appeared, in that moment, angelic, or maybe just beyond human, as one not wholly possessed by the present. In that moment she seemed capable of transcending the chasm of

Viga: Carved and decorated roof beam from original church at Socorro. *Image courtesy of Angie Browne.*

time between the mission's founding and the present; she seemed capable of touching and having a firm hold on each, of being an integral part of each. It was only a moment. But when she returned to us and again turned to have a look at the mission, she said, "It's such an amazing little treasure in this area."[40]

Much like the missions of San Antonio, the Presidio San Elizario had its beginnings in a different location. The Presidio de Nuestra Señora de las Caldas de Guajoquilla was founded in 1752 in what is today Jimenez, Mexico, in the northern state of Chihuahua.

In August 1765, King Charles III selected the Marqués de Rubí, a Spanish field marshal and knight commander of a noble family from Barcelona, to tour the Spanish establishments, from the interior of Nueva España to New Mexico and east Texas. The conditions all along the frontier of Spain's new territories had deteriorated to such a degree that the king demanded an official, third-party opinion on what should be done to shore up defenses. Rubí toured the regions beginning in March 1766 and, twenty-three months later, had completed his task. Perhaps obviously, his first journeys led him to the colleges of Zacatecas and Querétaro, to discover what the Franciscans' plans might be for the missions and presidios. Rubí then crossed the Rio Grande in the summer of 1767 in the El Paso region, trekked northward into New Mexico, took a circuitous route back through the Mexican interior, crossed again the Rio Grande and visited the presidio at San Sabá, passed through the Bejar territory and inspected those missions and presidios in the east before returning toward the capital in Mexico.

The report filed by Rubí, *Reglamento e Instrucción para los Presidios que se han de Formar en la Línea de Frontera de la Nueva España,* was stark and honest. In his opinion, as a soldier and field marshal, the missions and presidios of east Texas should be abandoned. Further, he recommended concentrating settlements at Santa Fe and San Antonio and studding the southernmost edge of the entire territory with presidios, at a distance of 120 miles (40 leagues) apart, from the bay at California to the delta of the Guadalupe River in Texas. Additionally, Rubí recommended an extensive and complete destruction of the Apache (Lipan) tribes, which were, he reported, the cause both of much destruction within the Spanish communities and excessive intertribal chaos.

The job of realigning the presidios and sweeping the Apaches from the territory fell to Hugh O'Connor (in Spanish, Hugo Oconór), an Irishman who had moved to Spain as a young man due to religious and political beliefs. O'Connor established a presidio in Arizona that would eventually become Tucson and also fortified the community at San Antonio. In order to prevent further Indian incursions into the Texas region from the east, O'Connor had the presidio at Los Adeas reinforced and restructured. As for the Apaches, O'Connor (known as the "Red Captain" for his hair and bloodlust) exacted heavy losses, killing hundreds and forcing thousands farther west.

The presidio of San Elizario (named for Saint Elzéar of Sabran, the famously devout Catholic patron saint of soldiers) was the location of the aforementioned San Lorenzo, where Otermín had convened his troops and New Mexican settlers after the 1680 revolt. At that time, the immediate area also held the much smaller, and now lost, mission of Nuestra Señora del Pilar y Gloriosa San José. After Vargas had retaken New Mexico, several of the previously displaced families returned to their former homes. Others decided to remain where they were; after all, the region was fertile and relatively calm, save the Apache raids. Among those staying behind was the Tiburcio Ortega family. Their land was expansive, and the region became known as the Hacienda de Los Tiburcios. In order to protect the Spanish as well as the Piro and Tigua tribes, the Spanish army decided to transfer the presidio of San Elceario from its location about ten leagues east of the Tiburcio family (the same presidio of Caldas de Guajoquilla) onto the land of the hacienda.

El Presidio de San Elceario was established in 1789, primarily due to O'Connor's restructuring efforts and his attempts to quell Apache deprivations. A chapel was added to the fortress for the soldiers' and their

San Elizario Presidio under reconstruction. *University of Texas at El Paso Library Special Collections Department, El Paso Herald Post Records.*

families' ecclesiastical needs. It is this structure, or the most recent incarnation, that still stands today. Some forty years after its construction, the chapel was yet another victim of the Rio Grande's raging temperament; in 1829, it was very nearly blotted from the landscape. A second chapel was built and was soon too small to nurture the growing population. The present building was founded in 1877, although it, too, has suffered its own distress. An electrical short in 1935 filled the church with smoke. As a response, the wooden ceiling was covered with tin, the walls were repainted and new chandeliers replaced the old. The bell tower is a later addition.

In all of its different guises, El Presidio de San Elceario has kept a watchful eye on the communities of Isleta and Socorro for centuries. Even today, the church serves the residents of the area, holding Mass on a regular, weekly schedule. During a recent visit in the early evening, the church, full of worshipers, appeared ethereal at blue dusk, with the stained-glass windows gleaming from the light within. A group of teenage girls was gathered just outside the entrance, practicing a dance routine for their local school. The courtyard directly in front of the building, a sort of community center where the whole neighborhood appears to gather no matter the day or occasion, was teeming with locals idly chatting.

San Elizario Presidio. *Image courtesy of author.*

Of the entire El Paso region, as concerns the missions and presidio, it can be said that the original intent of the settlements—to gather, protect and allow to flourish those who were in need of exactly that nourishment—has succeeded. In fact, it was this region that truly allowed Texas to become what it is today. As Anne Hughes wrote several decades ago:

> *Though the beginning of Texas is commonly associated with the small group of missions established by Massanet in 1680 on the Neches River in Eastern Texas, as a matter of fact, the true beginnings of what is now Texas are to be found in the settlements grouped along the Rio del Norte in the El Paso district.*[41]

CHAPTER 4

THE MISSIONS AND PRESIDIOS OF SAN ANTONIO

MISSION SAN ANTONIO DE VALERO

All of the missions in the San Antonio region tell a tale of journeying and purpose. Indeed, the same could be said of most of the missions within present-day Texas. However, the sites for the missions in this area were chosen for slightly different reasons than those around Goliad or El Paso. The missions at San Antonio were established with the definite purpose to succor and aid, while those in Goliad and El Paso were founded mostly to defend against and blockade French advancement or provide rest from retreat from hostile Native Americans, respectively.

As mentioned earlier, the initial Spanish settlements in the San Antonio area were the direct result of the efforts of Father Antonio de San Buenaventura y Olivares and then governor of Coahuila and Texas, Martin de Alarcón. The mission and presidio were established along the San Antonio River (Villa de Béxar or, as some sources have it, San Fernando de Béxar). The name "Béxar" was taken from a Spanish crusader from Béjar, Spain, the Duke of Béxar, who died attempting to defend Budapest. The aim of these institutions was in some ways similar to those established at El Paso: to offer rest and comfort to the missionaries, Indians and Spanish settlers. The difference being, of course, that no one was chasing the Spanish from the east, and those retreating were not exactly intent on trying to reclaim the region, as Otermín had imagined for the New Mexican refugees. Father Olivares's vision, since he first visited the region in 1709, had been to found missions along the fertile region of the San Antonio River system. With the abandonment of the east Texas missions, he saw his opportunity. What the Franciscan had envisioned was a rest area for those supplies, settlers, religious and soldiers traveling the obdurate Camino Real from the Mexican interior to *la terra andentro*. The new viceroy, Marqués de Valero, agreed with the padre and commissioned Alarcón in 1716 with the duty of constructing Father Olivares's vision.

Delays of over a year and a half (mainly due to bickering between Alarcón and Olivares—Olivares would request and Alarcón would ignore) terminated when Alarcón founded the San Antonio de Valero Mission in May 1718. A few days later, San Antonio de Béxar Presidio was established at San Pedro Springs. As will be remembered, these new fortifications were developed none too soon. In 1721, those people from the missions of east Texas were very glad to have these new stations to settle into. Otherwise, their trek would have taken several more months and hundreds of hard miles in order to cross the Rio Grande and obtain assistance.

The pilgrimage of the Spanish missions from east Texas to San Antonio is not as unusual a journey as one may suspect. The Villa de Béxar had been not only an aspiration for Father Olivares but was also something of a semi-luxurious necessity for the area's residents. The train of man, animal and supply reaching from Mexico into Texas had become constant. The trail had been struck, and there was nothing to halt the flow of supplies; now was the time merely for ordinary setbacks and delays. The Aguayo expedition had been more successful than anticipated. Settlers from the Canary Islands, Cuba and Galicia (northwestern Spain) were streaming in, and the San Antonio region was flourishing. Indeed, when France ceded Louisiana to Spain in 1762, with the Fontainebleau Treaty, trading all the land of the Mississippi River Valley and that stretching from the Appalachians to the Rockies, the need for any Spanish presidio or mission in east Texas became redundant. Additionally, Anglo immigration was increasing steadily. The more direct need, as the Franciscans came to view things, was to maintain a religious presence in this new, prospering territory.

Mission San Antonio de Valero had its beginnings on the south side of the Rio Grande in 1700. Initially, the mission had the name San Francisco Solano and was positioned very close to another, San Juan Bautista, in present-day Guerrero, Mexico, in the state of Coahuila. The Spanish authority then was none other than Diego Ramón; Fathers Olivares and Hidalgo were given charge of the missions. As we have seen, Fray Hidalgo was one to lead by example. His trust in his mission, his unyielding faith and his stalwart

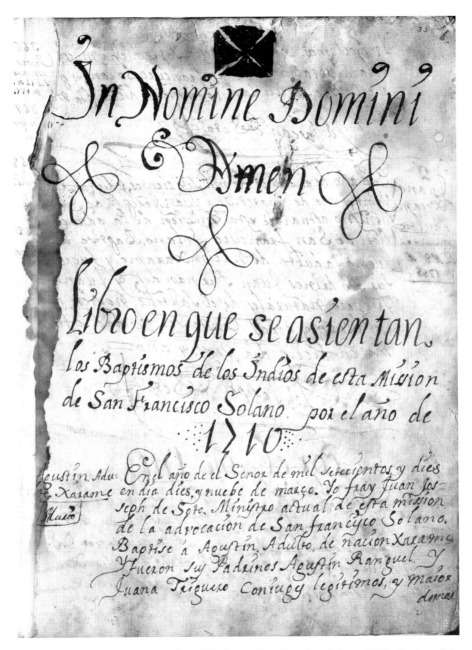

Front page of records document from Mission de San Francisco Solano, 1710. *Courtesy of the Catholic Archives at San Antonio. Not to be reproduced without the proper authorization of the archives.*

Sketch of Mission Valero, pre-1850. *Courtesy of Witte Museum, San Antonio, Texas.*

belief in his life's work attracted even the most contrary souls. Conversely, Father Olivares has been variously described as cantankerous or even brittle. Olivares knew exactly what his vocation was and held fast to the tenets of his faith. However, unlike Hidalgo, Olivares's patience was quickly worn thin by the recalcitrant attitudes of some of the natives with whom he worked. He longed for displacement, and when, after visiting the San Antonio region, he discovered a verdant, rich-soiled, water-blessed community, he knew where his next mission lay.

After requesting permission from the Marqués de Valero, Olivares wasted little time in transferring the Mission San Francisco Solano, along with a few of the faithful Jarame Indians at Solano, across the Rio Grande to the area of San Antonio. The mission was initially known as San Antonio de Padua, and then Olivares added the cognomen "de Valero" in honor of the viceroy who had granted the Franciscan permission for the mission's transfer.

At first, the mission was located on the west side of the San Antonio River. According to various sources, the mission complex was moved to the east side of the river sometime around 1724, and some two decades later, a more permanent construction, of stone and adobe, was begun. The population in the area quickly increased. Mission San Francisco Xavier de Naxera (Nájara) had been hastily founded in 1722 by Aguayo three miles south of Valero for a large confederacy of Coahuiltecan and Tonkawa tribes led by an Ervipiame chief named Juan Rodríguez. The Native Americans residing at that mission resettled at Valero, since the latter site proved much more comforting and protective. However, it appears Father Olivares's perception of Alarcón was shared by others, and this, at first, threatened the inception of the seedling mission effort. As Marlon Habig noted:

> *In a letter which he wrote on June 22, 1718, Fr. Olivares mentioned the fact that Alarcón had treated his Indian guide so badly that the latter had run away after they reached San Antonio and joined the Indians of the vicinity; and Alarcón had made the threat that if the Indians would not come to the mission, he would go in search of them and put them to the sword. That was no doubt one reason why the Indians did not come.*[42]

Nevertheless, it will be remembered that at this time Alarcón was ordered to assist the missions in east Texas that had been, for so long, in so desperate a situation. Recalling how anemic that assistance was, it would appear that Alarcón's greatest offering for the mission effort was his absence. During Alarcón's trip to the east, which lasted from September 1718 to January of the following year, Olivares persuaded a large number of Payaya and Pamaya Indians to settle at the Valero mission. The region was soon home to hundreds of Spanish settlers, Native American tribes and large herds of cattle, goats, sheep and horses. The land being well irrigated, it was producing an abundance of crops. Due to all of this, the San Antonio region was also becoming very attractive to those of a more furtive nature, and the mission's structure began to more closely resemble a fort than a center of worship. On the other hand, one contribution of Alarcón's should be mentioned. Habig notes that on his return to Valero from the east, Alarcón "brought along a bell that he had found on the site of the first mission of San Francisco which had been abandoned in 1693."[43] The mission and its environs flourished in a way that Father Olivares probably never imagined. As James Burke wrote, "Mission San Antonio de Valero prospered; and some of Texas' first and most successful missions were established there. San Antonio became the stronghold of Spanish occupation for the entire country."[44] It is regrettable that Olivares, aged and having suffered a broken leg, retired from San Antonio in 1720 and was never witness to the magnitude of his success. However, after his leg had healed, Olivares did oversee the transfer of the mission to its present location; it is assumed that he then retired to his old home, the Colegio de Querétaro.

The history of Mission San Antonio de Valero is exciting because it is complex. Again, due to the nature of its success, the area attracted not only

Mission Valero, "Alamo," late nineteenth century. *Courtesy of Witte Museum, San Antonio, Texas.*

more missions but also thousands of residents. However, the earliest forms of the mission little resemble what we recognize today as the Alamo.

When Father Olivares initially reestablished Mission San Francisco de Solano in the San Antonio region, the buildings were not constructed with a sense of permanency. Initially built of timber and thatch, like those in east Texas, the mission was moved no fewer than three times from near the San Pedro Springs area before nestling into its present spot. In fact, within only the past few years (beginning around 2013), archaeological teams with the city of San Antonio have discovered what some are referring to as the "possible first site of Mission San Antonio de Valero." This site is directly on—or under—the Christopher Columbus Italian Society building complex. Core samples have found Spanish colonial–era trade beads, some pottery sherds from the period and even some iron bits dating to the period. However, because construction of the society buildings and the parking lot may have disturbed or displaced some artifacts, more work is needed to confirm the hypothesis that Father Olivares first set up his mission at this site.

Wherever that first site was located, a hurricane-force storm in 1724 destroyed most of the existing mission structures. And, yet again, European diseases decimated the native populace in 1739–40. Undeterred, the missionaries laid the cornerstone of today's "Alamo Church" on May 8, 1744. The original work bears little resemblance to what stands today.

100

According to Adina de Zavala, the first attempt at a permanent structure was a "pretty church with its twin towers, arched roof, and graceful dome…entirely finished about 1757."[45] Indeed, it appears from the records that the architectural plan for Mission San Antonio de Valero was very ambitious. The church, as seen today, is just slightly more than a third the size of what the Spanish had envisioned. If it had been completed to its full extent, the façade of the church itself would have greatly resembled Concepción, with twin towers, one on either side of the main doors, and a domed nave. Additionally, there was to be a third story, wherein an icon of Our Lady of the Immaculate Conception was to be placed. Today's church façade shows only four niches, two on the first floor and two on the second, where statues of other saints once stood. On the first floor, to each side of the portal doors, St. Dominic's sculpture used to stand in the niche at the right and a sculpture of St. Francis to the left. Above, on the second floor, statues of St. Clare and St. Margaret held positions in those niches. Jacinto Quirarte points out, "According to an anonymous traveler (1837), the sculptures in the niches flanking the doorway of the main portal were still in place a year after the famous battle of the Alamo."[46] Franciscan inspection tours noted the beauty of these early guises of the mission's façade. Father Saenz in 1772 and then Father Mofi in 1778 both wrote detailed reports on the originality and creativity of the stonework as well as the overall appearance. Sadly, due to what Father Morfi described as the stupidity of the builder, much of this early work literally collapsed in on itself, leaving only the lower portion of the church as we know it today. (Morfi's name is a Hispanicized form of "Murphy." Like O'Connor, Father Morfi was indeed born in Galicia, but to Irish parents who had left Ireland for the same religious reasons as had O'Connor and so many others.) Interestingly, though, on the keystone, located just over the middle of the main doors, the monogram of the Virgin Mary still maintains its original spot: AVMR (*Ave María*, Latin for "Hail, Mary").

The extent of the mission's grounds was expansive. Burke succinctly defined the mission's extended area a few decades ago:

> *The original fortifications which surrounded the mission and pueblo had little in common with the timid walls one sees today at Alamo Plaza. The original extended north across Houston Street enclosing some of the plot of the Federal Building, and south to Crockett Street; it reached east to beyond Nacogdoches Street, and swept westward across Alamo Plaza to the banks of the San Antonio River (which at that time ran parallel to the wall).*

Reconstructed "Alamo," early twentieth century. *Courtesy of Witte Museum, San Antonio, Texas.*

This, then, was one of the largest of all Texas missions....It was also one of the best fortified.[47]

Once the mission had assumed its present location, more permanent construction began. Having learned their lesson from earlier structural failures, friars quarried rock from the nearby river. Indeed, a branch of the San Antonio River once flowed directly behind the south wall of the complex, allowing for direct access to both the bedrock and a water supply for washing and bathing. A well was dug within the walled perimeter in case of siege, and an *acequia* (aqueduct) was dug to help direct the river's flow to the crops and livestock. In fact, this acequia was in use well into the nineteenth century and had, by that time, acquired the name "Alamo Madre." After the city began to expand, the rock used for the aqueduct was pulled up and used as construction material.

A *convento* was built (part of which remains today along the "barracks" wall), rooms were constructed to house work areas for looms and ironwork and a granary and other areas for storage and tile manufacture were added around the grounds. In addition, a ranch, La Mora, was included just south of the mission, its name presumably a nod to the wild blackberries in the area. The expanse of the mission's surroundings speaks not only to the Franciscans' aspirations but also to the growth of the area. This new mission was to house the religious, soldiers and Spanish families, as well as Native Americans from the Zanas, Cocos, Tovs, Karankawa and Payayes tribes. In time, several other native tribes—according to some sources over one hundred other groups—would also reside near the complex. And, as mentioned before, the Franciscans, in an effort to minimize potential infighting among the tribes, encouraged the natives to intermarry. These marriages, well documented among the several and meticulous records kept by the friars, had the benefit of keeping the couples and their families attached to the mission system. Still, even with such a relatively large number of personnel, resources and attention, the mission at Valero was never structurally completed, the best-laid plans of its architects never fully realized.

Mission Valero prospered for the next few decades. Despite frequent—and often severe—Apache raids, the mission held its own. As with most of the Spanish effort in Texas, the decline of Valero began from within. The expulsion of the Jesuits caused considerable concern for all the church's work in the Americas. For some time, the Jesuits cared for the missions in lower (*baja*) and upper (*alta*) California. Upon their removal to Europe, the priests from the college at Querétaro were asked to take over the maintenance of the Jesuit missions in the west. Of course, they complied, but they were now obligated to, in turn, request that the priests from the college of Zacatecas receive care of the missions in Texas that had, until that time, been under the supervision of Querétaro. So, in 1773, the missions of the San Antonio area became the province of the college of the Zacatecan missionaries. Over the next twenty years, the city of San Antonio flourished; as it did, the Native

"Alamo" as U.S. Army supply depot. *Courtesy of Witte Museum, San Antonio, Texas.*

American population at Valero decreased. So it was that in 1793, at the request of the college of Zacatecas, the Mission Valero and its lands were secularized. The religious obligations were handed off to the church of San Fernando. (During the construction of this church [1738–48], the Spanish families took Mass at Valero.) Valero's land, animals and other resources were doled out among the Native Americans of the area. What followed was the gradual disappearance of the original structure. The cathedral of San Fernando was now in operation, and many of the citizens obtained their religious edification at this building rather than the nearby mission.

Until now, the term "Alamo" has been avoided, because that moniker is a later addition to the story described thus far. As Jacinto Quirarte wrote:

> *The former mission has been known as the Alamo since 1802, when troops from Mexico were quartered there. They belonged to the Second Flying Company* [Compania Valante] *of San Carlos de Parras del Alamo. The name of the former mission actually became the Pueblo San José y*

Santiago del Alamo. The Alamo served as a military fortress from 1802 to 1836, when the last of the sieges between the Mexican army and Anglo-American settlers took place.[48]

As noted, Mission Valero was never fully completed. Now, in the nineteenth century, possession of the sprawling property began to cause issues within the San Antonio community. However, the mission was swallowed up by the growth of the city. Gradually, only the chapel and portions of the defensive walls were to be seen. As Susan Schoelwer notes:

Much of the mission compound now lies buried beneath city streets and buildings and is revealed only occasionally and fragmentarily by archaeological fieldwork. San Antonio de Valero lost its identity as an integrated complex during the nineteenth century. The United States Army occupied the site in 1846, provoking a three-way title controversy with the city of San Antonio and the Catholic Church.[49]

It was during the army's occupation of the site that, in 1850, the now-famous gable atop the chapel was added. It is not difficult for one to discern the line separating the lower, original stonework from the newer, restored portion. Luckily, though, the original section left to us is a wonderful example of the Franciscans' dedication to not only their fortitude but their artistry as well.

The realization that care needed to be taken in preserving the Valero Mission began in the late nineteenth century. For several years, the controversy centered on the convento, presumably because it was plain-looking and, from a mercantile perspective, an obstacle to progress. Luckily, preservation efforts succeeded, mainly due to Clara Driscoll, who, in 1905, bought the property after much dickering with the owners of a large, two-story business that had been built directly next to the chapel (and on the mission's grounds). She turned its management over to the Daughters of the Republic of Texas, which underwent its own troubles in trying to restore the mission's grounds. However, it was this organization that claimed right to the land surrounding the church and began removing the non-historic structures in the early twentieth century. As with so many iconic structures around the country, the Works Progress Administration (WPA) was responsible for much of the work of restoring the mission's walls in the 1930s.

To try to comment or even explain the long and complex journey of Mission Valero from 1900 to the present day would require a book in itself,

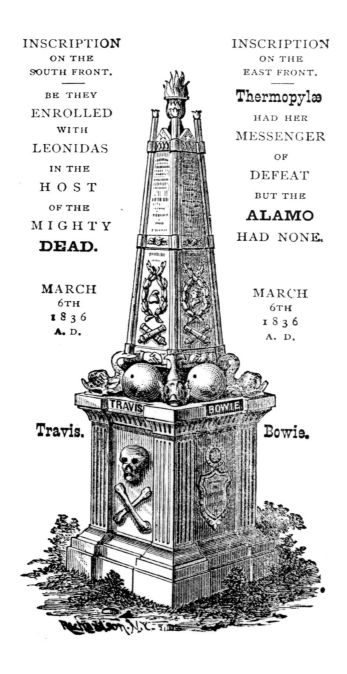

INSCRIPTION
ON THE
SOUTH FRONT.

BE THEY
ENROLLED
WITH
LEONIDAS
IN THE
HOST
OF THE
MIGHTY
DEAD.

MARCH
6TH
1836
A. D.

INSCRIPTION
ON THE
EAST FRONT.

Thermopylæ
HAD HER
MESSENGER
OF
DEFEAT
BUT THE
ALAMO
HAD NONE.

MARCH
6TH
1836
A. D.

Travis.

TRAVIS

BOWIE

Bowie.

Detail of "Alamo" monument. *Courtesy of Witte Museum, San Antonio, Texas.*

for the story is a labyrinth of opposition and politicization. Let it suffice to mention that the "Long Barrack" was restored into a museum in 1968, when San Antonio hosted the Hemisfair. Restoration work continued until very recently; in a sense, though, it is ongoing. As recently as 2011, the property was owned by the Texas General Land Office. It is the only mission of the five in the San Antonio region that is owned by the State of Texas. As of 2015, Mission San Antonio de Valero has been placed on the UNESCO World Heritage List.

MISSION SAN JOSÉ Y MIGUEL DE AGUAYO

Two years after the first establishment of Mission San Antonio de Valero, Father Antonio Margil de Jesus, the custos, or president, of the college at Zacatecas, founded the Mission San José y Miguel de Aguayo along the San Antonio River, in 1720. According to some sources, this mission was established for two reasons. First, Native American tribes (the Pampopas and Pastías, chief among a few others) in the San Antonio region were inimical toward those at Valero and requested from Aguayo a mission of their own. Second, the new mission provided solace for the exodus of those Indians and Spanish from the east after the French "attack" (the "Chicken War"). Its location, dictated by Spanish law to keep warring tribes a distance from one another, was just over three leagues south from Valero. Once again, Father Isidro Felix de Espinosa in his *Cronica* says that the founding of San José was, in the minds of the Franciscans, at least, a direct result of the French advance into eastern Texas:

> [In] *the year of (17)16 and (17)17 three missions were founded, which still exist today in the middle of the Texas* [area] *and are in the care of the said College (Zacatecas). When we all retreated due to the invasion of the French, the Mission San José was founded on the banks of the San Antonio River, which* [mission] *still remains.*[50]

Similar to Valero, San José was moved twice in the San Antonio River area before being permanently founded at its present area in 1740. As with all the missions in the San Antonio region, the river's course was determinate in these missions' establishment—that is, a mission's great need for a constant freshwater source was essential in deciding the location.

The name of Mission San José y Miguel de Aguayo is a simple matter. Saint Joseph, the biblical husband of Mary, is the patron saint, perhaps strangely, of the deathbed, as well as the rose, which is noted as an emblem of the relationship between himself and his wife. Saint Michael is, of course, the archangel who will have the final dominion and victory over Satan at the end of our time. His omnipresent authority, as we saw at El Paso's Socorro Mission, is an indispensable presence among the faithful. The inclusion of "Aguayo" (as with Valero) is an honorific for the Marqués de San Miguel de Aguayo, who granted permission to Father Margil for the mission's founding.

Uncharacteristically of the Spanish authorities at this time, the first records of baptisms, marriages and other rites are lost. The first accountings at San José attribute approximately 230 Native Americans, from several tribes, to this new mission. The care of these persons and of the church was handed to Father Miguel Núñez de Haro, the same friar who had tried to take the desperately needed supplies to the missions in east Texas but was forced to leave them hidden in a grove of trees due to the impossibility of crossing the swollen Trinity River. Father Núñez moved Mission San José twice, the first time most likely for better irrigation and the second to higher ground, less than half a league distant, after yet another epidemic ravaged the populace in 1739. It was after this horror that the Franciscans began to build San José with urgency.

Mission San José y San Miguel de Aguayo, as it is referred to today, was begun when Father Pedro Ramírez de Arellano was placed in charge of the mission in 1759. As with most Franciscan keepers of this mission, Father Ramírez was president of the college at Zacatecas during this time. Construction of the present site was begun in 1768, and many of the sacred items from the first church were repurposed for the new one. As Quirarte observed:

> *The main altarpiece of the new church had a sculpture of St. Joseph in an "old niche" above a carved and gilded tabernacle. Its diadem and staff were both made of silver. The niche in which the St. Joseph was placed had a small taffeta valance and another of printed cotton with a fringe. Both were trimmed with lace where they were tacked onto the niche. Listed for the first time were a small baldachin used to crown the altar and inside it a sculpture of the Crucified Christ with a base inlaid with bone.*[51]

As with Mission Valero, now only a league and a half north, the compound of Mission San José was expansive and constructed with a unique expression

Façade of Mission San José y Miguel. *Image courtesy of author.*

of permanency. The mission not only included a marvelous church with a two-story convent for the religious, but the surrounding grounds comprised living quarters for the Spanish guards, an armory, apartments for the neophytes, a granary, cells for carpenters, looms and other textile works and even a space for the conversion of sugar cane into molasses. According to Burke, this latter production was "the first record of sugar being made from sugarcane in Texas." It is no wonder that Mission San José has earned the sobriquet "The Queen of the Missions." The façade, with its single belfry to the right of the portal doors, is unique among the missions of the region. Likewise, the elaborate detailing of the sculptures around and above the façade's doors has been variously described as elegant, wonderful, rich, exquisite, a joy forever and daring in its ornamentation. Indeed, even behind the church's domed nave is a cloistered walkway that surely must have offered those within a sense of calm and strength as they walked from Mass to the day's chores. The arches that cover this path are so perfectly aligned as to remind one of the flying buttresses that spread behind Notre Dame. It seems that little was spared in the way of accoutrement for this new mission. As Burke notes:

> *Everything was arranged for the comfort of the new Christians. At this modern mission another first for Texas was achieved, the wonders of which would have startled the cattle barons of a much later era. There was a swimming pool for the neophytes. The water was brought from the river by means of a gravity canal that flowed along the houses, from there into the pool, and out into the adjoining fields, where it was not wasted but used for irrigation purposes. Near the soldiers' quarters there was a second swimming pool, an early precedent for segregation practices.*[52]

The church at San José is as impressive today as it was in the late eighteenth century. As with the presidio at La Bahía, the church at San José withstood the majority of man's and nature's aggression. The defensive, enclosing walls have been reconstructed, as has the old mill just outside the north wall. Even the south tower, which collapsed in the early twentieth century, was promptly pieced back together (an effort that included the arduous restoration of that portion of the original fresco that can still be seen today). Through it all, the church has remained relatively stable and intact. The ornate carvings around the portal doors and the sacristy window, in particular, are awe-inspiring. Marvelous examples of the Baroque period include the lavish styling of the roses (symbolic of the bond between Joseph and Mary) surrounding the sacristy window; the scalloped enclave niches both under the saints' statues and above some of the interior doorways and fonts; and the lavish use of the acanthus leaf (which can also be seen adorning the capitals of ancient Roman Corinthian columns). The identity of the artist who, in fact, sculpted the window and portal entrance has become somewhat contentious in the last several years.

Mission San José, showing dome and "Rose Window." *Image courtesy of author.*

For well over two centuries, this extraordinary illustration of masonry has been attributed to Pedro Huízar, a Spanish sculptor, surveyor and civic employee of the Spanish colonial government. Recently this writer had the pleasure of speaking with Vincent Huízar, a sixth-generation descendant of Don Pedro Huízar. Vincent Huízar had brought along a number of documents indicating his family has lived in the immediate area of the San José Mission since the mid-eighteenth century, when his great-great-great-grandfather Pedro was employed as the chief architect of the mission. Among the many papers and documents were several denoting accounts for building materials that were either requisitioned or itemized by Pedro Huízar and signed with, at the time, the common rubric, or flourish, that accompanied all signatures. Vincent Huízar's papers also consisted of several items relating to other family members from the nineteenth century. Among these were two "Company Muster Roll" forms from 1862 wherein both a Juan and Vicente Huízar were enlisted in Company B, Fourth Battalion, Arizona Brigade (also called, at times, Davidson's Battalion Texas Cavalry) of the Confederate army. The documents indicate that both young men were enrolled on the very same day and for the same duration of service: September 20 to December 31, 1862. The gravestone on the grounds of

San José marks, in fact, this same Huízar—Juan Dedios Huízar—who was one of the grandsons of Pedro. Huízar was so intimate with Mission San José that not only is the mission his final resting place, but, according to Vincent Huízar, he was born in the mission's granary in 1833.

The Huízar family has traced their lineage to Pedro Huízar's birth in Spain in 1740. During those years of Don Pedro's life, he was exceedingly active in the Spanish colonization of the Texas region. Having arrived in Nueva España in 1774 (most likely arriving at Vera Cruz, as so many others did), Don Pedro was a "servant" of the Franciscans and was put to work as a sculptor and carpenter in the missions both in the San Antonio area and those at Goliad as well. In addition to those incredible stone carvings at San José, Don Pedro is also believed to have had a hand in the stonework and carpentry at Concepción; conducted land surveying around Valero, San José, Concepción and Espíritu Santo; helped itemize materials at all the region's missions after their secularizations; and was even the municipal judge for the San José area in his later years. Perhaps not surprisingly, the Spanish government awarded Don Pedro with, according to Vincent Huízar, two hundred acres of land at each of the missions at which he

The "Rose Window." *Image courtesy of author.*

was employed. Some of this land was bequeathed to his family and, again according to Huízar but easily verified when observing the forged signatures of Don Pedro, other tracts were taken in what could only be considered a land grab in the chaos after the Civil War. Indeed, Mary Maverick, in her famous memoir about her family's early life in the San Antonio area, recalls that, in 1838, her family lived in a home owned by the Huízars. "The house we rented belonged to the Huisars [sic]. Huisar, the ancestor, carved the beautiful doors for the San Jose Mission—he had quite a number of workmen under him and was employed several years in the work."[53]

No one can be sure whether Maverick was referring to just the mission's portal doors (which, from accounts, were wooden, meticulously carved and meticulously stolen off their hinges sometime between 1880 and 1890) or the entire structure of the doorway. The latter could include the fantastic stonework around the doors. In either case, it is certain that Don Pedro and his family were in residence in the San José region from almost the beginning of the Franciscans' work at Mission San José and that Don Pedro and his sons and grandsons were very involved with the construction and daily maintenance of the missions in the regions of San Antonio and Goliad.

The other artist given credit for the extravagant carvings at San José is Antonio Salazar. According to Schuetz-Miller, he is listed in the early records of the mission as the "Master Mason and Architect of San Jose." The same source has Huízar listed as "Carpenter of San José y San Miguel de Aguayo and San Fernando de Austria, Surveyor and Political Figure."[54] Although Schuetz-Miller's information is gleaned from both archival and published sources, it seems uncertain that Salazar should be listed as the mason responsible for the Rose Window and the ornamentation of the portal doors simply because he is listed once as "maestro," or teacher/ instructor. It was common in this time to refer to a worker as "servant," as in "servant of the Lord," or "teacher" (maestro), as in "instructor for others in the trade." From the existing records, it appears that Pedro Huízar arrived in the San Antonio area a few years before Salazar, sometime in 1775, from Aguascalientes, Mexico—a city well known, both then and now, as a haven for artists. As a young man, Pedro Huízar would have seen and studied the grand Baroque churches in Aguascalientes, and it is not difficult to recognize the influence this cultural center must have had on the young artist in training. The standard Baroque imagery of angels, acanthus leaves and flowers was inherent to the genre, and Huízar brought this to the New World.

Gravestone of Juan Huísar, San José Mission. *Image courtesy of author.*

The other reasons for crediting Huízar with the window and other decoration at San José are circumstantial, but together they are compelling. Pedro arrived, as mentioned, in 1775 in the San Antonio region. The first mention of Antonio Salazar dates to 1781, where he and his wife are listed as godparents to one of Huízar's daughters. The present-day ancestor of Pedro Huízar has the benefit of oral tradition within his own family, a family that has lived within a mile or two of the mission for over 250 years. When one considers that Homer's *Iliad* and *Odyssey* were transmitted orally for a couple of centuries before being written down, it is not difficult to imagine that, within one's own family, a single story can remain uncorrupted for approximately the same amount of time. And a 1936 report on the Mission San José y San Miguel de Aguayo completed by the National Park Service as part of a Historic American Buildings Survey reads: "Architect: Pedro Huisar [*sic*] and Builder: The Franciscan friars and Indians under the direction of Pedro Huisar."

A portion of the Huízar family's tradition is also very compelling to the story. First, Vincent Huízar says the story about the Rose Window is true—it was named for a young woman named Rosa Monterrey. She was Pedro's betrothed but died when her ship sank off the coast of Vera Cruz as she traveled from Spain for their marriage. The window became an offering of his love for the young woman who was denied the satisfaction of seeing this token of his affections—the woman who was lost both to the sea and her lover. Then, as Vincent Huízar mentioned, in the early excavations of the 1930s, human remains were found buried just inside the church under the sacristy window. These remains were reburied another six feet down and left directly below where they had been found; Vincent claims that this is his ancestor. Perhaps most compelling of all is Huízar's assertion that in the 1960s, while watching restorers work on the Rose Window, one of the workers exclaimed that the tool markings on and around the window had been created with woodworking tools, those of a carpenter, not a rock mason. I asked Huízar one last time, for clarity and certainty's sake, whether he was sure of his claims about this ancestor. Had Pedro Huízar really been the progenitor of all this masterful work around the missions? He smiled, then laughed; he has done his research, he stated. Besides, he added, "We didn't start this story just fifty years ago!"[55]

In any case, the work at San José is an incredible demonstration of effort, determination and skill. It is a blessing for all of us that the artist's craft has been maintained through not only the trials of erosion and neglect but also the puerile glee some soldiers in the nineteenth century took in using the statues, and other focal points in the masonry, as target practice.

In 1777, Fray Juan Agustin Morfi made a formal visit through the entire region with Teodoro de Croix, the newly elected commandant general of the Provincias Internas. This was an enormous and recently regulated stretch of land that included Coahuila, Texas, New Mexico, Sonora and both Baja and Alta California. It was reasoned that such a grouping would improve the political machinations of the region. Morfi, visiting San José in

Altar at San José. *Image courtesy of author.*

January 1778, documented this expedition in his *History of Texas*, a seminal work focused not only on the missions and their conditions but also on the countryside and the several and various Native American tribes with which his group came into contact. At San José, Morfi identified over twenty such tribes of neophytes, describing how the evangelical work of the Franciscans was hampered by the many dialects spoken among the natives. Nevertheless, Father Morfi was much impressed by the quality of the work at the mission, both religious and temporal. Morfi wrote that one of his own countrymen, as it were, took a hand in establishing the permanent structure we see today: "The corner stone was laid by Hugo O'Connor on May 19, 1768." Further, Morfi adds that Mission San José is one of the most extraordinary he has seen in his tenure: "It is, in truth, the first mission in America, not in point of time, but in point of beauty, plan and strength, so that there is not a presidio along the entire frontier line that can compare with it."

Morfi also comments on the masonry work on the church's façade, noting what type of stone was used and its source: limestone quarried from the riverbank near Mission Concepción. He adds that the façade is very costly, due to the elaborate decoration and saints' statues. But he seems to have more admiration for the work's artistry than the expense when he writes, "No one could have imagined that there were such good artists in so desolate a place." This is an interesting comment, since the Franciscans had paid for the travel, training and importation of their own workers. However, it is probable that Morfi is commenting on the work of Huízar's Indian students.

Father Morfi describes Mission San José in great detail, from its size and inventory to all things necessary for the Franciscans' ecclesiastical efforts. Near the end of his report on this mission, he does, at last, delve into not only the heart of the mission's purpose but, in fact, the purpose for himself and all his brothers:

> *The mission was founded with Pampas, Mesquites, and Pastias to which later were added Camanas, Tacames, Cannes, Aquastallas, and Juanes. These Indians are today well instructed and civilized and know how to work very well at their mechanical trades and are proficient in some of the arts. They speak Spanish perfectly with the exception of those who are daily brought in from the wood by the zeal of the missionaries. Many play the harp, the violin and the guitar as well, sing well and dance the same dances as the Spaniards....* [The Indians] *who enjoy so much plenty, and whose mission is in opulence, thanks to the labors and exertions of Fray Pedro Ramirez de Arellano of the college of Nuestra Señora de Guadalupe of Zacatecas.*[56]

Statue of Father Margil, now at San José. *Image courtesy of Angie Browne.*

Of the mission's most famous piece of sculpture, Marion Habig notes that "Fr. Morfi does not mention the so-called Rose Window, which is the exterior ornamental frame of the sacristy's south window. It was probably sculptured after the church had been completed in 1782."[57] In that same year, the number of American Indians gathered at the Mission San José was less than half of what it had been just twenty years prior. The records indicate that in 1768, over 350 neophytes enjoyed the comfort and shelter of the mission. By the year 1789, that number had fallen to roughly 140, most likely due to yet another outbreak of smallpox or buboes (*nanaguates*), the swelling of the lymph nodes, typically of the top inner thigh, caused by either bubonic plague, syphilis, gonorrhea or tuberculosis.

During these few decades of the mission's growth, the area of San Antonio, just a few miles north, had been growing exponentially. The cathedral at San Fernando and the chapel of Valero had become the nuclei wherein immigrants gathered and from which the town branched out. There was strength in numbers, and even though the town experienced many and severe Indian attacks, those who chose to settle there found the region very favorable for their daily needs and future ambitions. For most of these, that ambition lay with acquiring land and raising herds of cattle, horses, sheep and/or goats. Each mission had its own *rancheria* where it kept its herd for the neophytes, and the community was also beginning to square off land for its own commercial interests. Perhaps obviously, all of these herds attracted attention; there was a great deal of money to be made in either raising or stealing these animals. Governor Teodoro de Croix realized this after his inspection tour with Father Morfi. And, since his duty to the crown was not insubstantially fiscal, his recommendation was to issue an order that claimed "all unbranded cattle to be government property and imposed a tax of four *reales* (one half a peso) for every head of unbranded cattle taken or killed by anyone, including the missions. The result was that the once opulent missions were impoverished."[58]

Needless to say, all the missions in the San Antonio area suffered because of this mandate. Before, the missions had not only sustained themselves but shared their surplus with each other and whomever else was in need. Now, with government regulations and an ever-increasing and independent populace, the need for the mission's assistance was waning. Further, those Native Americans who had begun their initial Christian training at the mission soon found that there was work in town—their Europeanization was completed by leaving the mission's grounds to become a part of the larger community.

Between the years 1768 and 1794, the number of neophytes at Mission San José waxed and waned, but with an overall gradual and steady decline. As this was occurring in the region, Mission San Antonio de Valero was secularized in 1793. The next year, the other four missions were "partially secularized." In all instances, Pedro Huízar was charged with taking inventories and surveying the properties. And, in 1796, Huízar was made *alcalde*, or mayor, of San José, even though, apart from the religious, the total population of Native Americans at the site was in the single digits. Coincidentally, Huízar's son José Antonio held the same position until 1819. For the missions in the San Antonio area, the nineteenth century was a tumultuous era, particularly the first half. The secularization of the missions was the first step in their decline. As the number of neophytes diminished, so, too, did government interest in supporting them financially.

Icon of Virgin Mary of Guadalupe at San José. *Image courtesy of author.*

Father Bernardino Vallejo wrote the last official report on the missions of the area, which he delivered in 1815. Father Vallejo told how the Mission San José had a population of just over one hundred persons, almost exactly half being Indian and the other Spanish.

Over the next decade, the four missions along the San Antonio River—San José, Concepción, Espada and Capistrano—were completely secularized by the New Mexican authority. In 1820, Father José Antonio Diaz de León, who had been in charge of the latest evangelical effort, Mission Nuestra Señora del Refugio, was transferred to San José. For four years he frustratingly tried to retain the support of the college at Zacatecas. Because the New Mexican government had incorporated Texas with Coahuila into a single state, secularization orders were completed. And so, on February 29, 1824, all four of the missions in the San Antonio River basin were officially offered to the local religious personnel.

Following this, the missions' possession changed hands as often as the political climate in the region changed. After Texas's independence in 1836, the diocese in charge was in New Orleans. Next came a transfer to Galveston

Left: "Rose Window" before restoration. *Courtesy of Witte Museum, San Antonio, Texas.*

Below: Original fresco at Mission San José. *Image courtesy of author.*

and then, finally, in 1874 the diocese of San Antonio was created and took charge. The following sixty years witnessed several differing organizations' occupation of the church at San José, the one building on the property that had withstood the years of inattention. With each new administration, some reconstruction efforts were made. An order of Benedictines arrived near midcentury and stayed about a decade. Next came the Holy Cross Fathers, and finally—and perhaps more simply—the local diocese entered. However, the buildings fell almost to ruins throughout the era. As Habig wrote:

> While divine services were held at San José more or less continuously since 1840…the walls of the mission square, with the Indian houses, disappeared. The vaulted roof of the granary collapsed. The old friary, too, became roofless. A part of the north wall of the church fell down on December 10, 1868; and the dome with the greater part of the roof crashed on December 25, 1874, while midnight services were going on in the sacristy.[59]

All of the San Antonio missions were used during the nineteenth century by various religious persons, the local community or others just passing through. One of the latter was John Russell Bartlett, who, in the mid-1800s, traveled through the Southwest taking notes and making sketches of the remnants of all the Spanish missions he encountered. His travel narratives are some of the best of the genre from that period. In the mid-1850s, Bartlett crossed into the San Antonio area and rested at San José. He noted:

> The most perfect portion of the church is an oval window in the sacristy which is surrounded with scrolls and wreath-work of exceeding grace and beauty.…It [the church] is seldom used for religious purposes; as the Mexicans of the neighborhood are poor, and cannot often afford the fifty dollars charged by the San Antonio priests for officiating.[60]

What Bartlett offers us is the opportunity to glance into the local society for what it truly was at this time. The churches beyond the vicinity of San Antonio were suffering from neglect of more than one sort. From no other source is this kind of information available: personal, direct and jarringly honest.

Restoration efforts at San José began almost as soon as history would allow. Once Mexico had separated itself from Spain and Texas gained independence from Mexico, there followed the requisite period of calm, a gathering of breath before the next moves. Habig describes the efforts made in the early twentieth century, restorations he describes as work that "has been the work of many minds and hearts, of individuals as well as organizations and societies."[61] He writes that some work was done to the church around 1917 but that it was not until the Franciscans returned in 1931 that the decision was made to have the roofless church completely restored.

Evidently, the church's reconstruction was satisfactory, because in the middle portion of the century attentions turned to the other areas of the complex. Habig writes that in 1924, a San Antonio Conservation Society was formed. It turned its focus to the north side of the mission square and had re-roofed the granary by 1933. Unlike the presidio at Goliad, the rock forming the walls surrounding the compound that comprises the Indians' and soldiers' quarters was not harvested from another antique, dilapidated structure. It was quarried from the original site along the river and, like the Acropolis in Athens, was taken from whatever detritus was found in the field on-site. Additionally, a San Antonio restoration company not only resupplied the rock needed for more current restoration but has also helped with the subsequent maintenance. Habig tells us that "the County of Béxar restored the walls and Indian quarters on the west, south, and east sides of the square in 1932."[62]

San José south tower. *Image courtesy of author.*

Quirarte is ever mindful of the old statuary and, like tracking the movement of an ancient manuscript, gives great detail about the journeys of these icons. Many of them are to be seen at the small museums within each mission still today. Of the church as a whole, he is somewhat reticent when he writes, "The sacristy doorway was restored in 1949."[63]

Due to the porous nature of the native limestone, water is the constant enemy of the missions. Beginning in 2009, several million dollars were raised to pay

Detail of St. Michael, altar at San José. *Image courtesy of author.*

restoration and reconstruction teams to support and correct what nature had eroded. This work is, paradoxically, both completed and ongoing. While the architects, masons and carpenters worked tirelessly for several years to complete their respective projects, the desire to use techniques and methods inherent to the period demands that these same entities remain on guard for any further damage.

In the 1960s and '70s, archaeological work unearthed original foundation stones along what was the Indians' quarters, as well as other artifacts from the colonial period. In 1941, the mission became both a state and national historical site. By 1978, all the missions had been incorporated into the San Antonio Missions National Historic Park. Then, beginning in 2008, Father David Garcia, who had been the rector at San Fernando Cathedral and was responsible for that historic site's restoration from 1995 to 2008, was asked by then Archbishop Gomez to restore the four missions. San José was brought to the condition we see today. Perhaps the most intriguing and rewarding aspect of all the monies raised and work expended is that Mission San José y San Miguel de Aguayo was included as a UNESCO World Heritage Site in 2015.

MISSION NUESTRA SEÑORA DE LA PURÍSIMA CONCEPCIÓN DE ACUÑA

Of the several missions in the San Antonio area, four were originally built in another region of the state and then transferred for financial and political reasons. Only Mission San Antonio de Valero holds the distinction of being solely indigenous to the region.

The Mission Nuestra Señora de la Purísima Concepción de los Hainai was first established in east Texas in 1716 for the college at Querétaro for the Ainay Indians, part of the Tejas confederacy. It was this mission that Father Espinosa had chosen for his headquarters, and it was from here that Espinosa wrote so much of his *Cronica* detailing the history of the Franciscans' work in the region. In fact, Father Espinosa's writings are so extensive and rich that he was given the moniker "El Julio Cesar de la Fé en Nueva España" (the Julius Caesar of the Faith in New Spain). It was also Espinosa, along with the other missionaries and the Native Americans to whom they were attending, who had to suffer through those two years of want and need while waiting for the anemic supply effort of Alarcón in 1718. In this year, the mission attracted the cognomen of "de Agreda," for the "Lady in Blue," María de Jesús de Ágreda.

Subsequently, due to the French and Spanish War of 1719 (resulting in the "Chicken War"), the missionaries and soldiers of the missions made a retreat toward the newly established San Antonio region. Waiting here for two years, the same group of religious returned to east Texas as part of the Aguayo expedition in 1721. As mentioned previously, this expedition not only reestablished those missions that had been abandoned but also instituted a new presidio near present-day Robeline, Louisiana. Nevertheless, these new missions in the east did not long enjoy their prosperity, for while the Franciscans did their best to reach out to the Native Americans in the Tejas group, their efforts were still, to some degree, maintained by the crown's purse, and it was not the missionaries who could lessen its strings.

In 1724, General Pedro de Rivera y Villalón was sent on an inspection tour of the defenses of the frontier beginning in New Mexico and stretching to east Texas. In 1727, he arrived in the eastern territory and, having made his notations, began the trek back, arriving in New Mexico in 1728. Rivera's recommendations were simple and focused: the presidios of Nuestra Señora de Loreto at La Bahía and of Nuestra Señora de los Dolores de los Tejas should be abandoned. Rivera also recommended a reduction in the number of troops at the presidio of Los Adaes. His ideas were accepted (not surprising, as the plan saved a substantial amount of money), and in

Mission Concepción, nineteenth century. *Courtesy of Witte Museum, San Antonio, Texas.*

1729, the Presidio de los Tejas was closed. This loss of protection did not sit well with the Franciscans left at the east Texas missions, and they gathered to draft their own letter to the viceroy. They asked for the presidio to be returned to the area. If the viceroy would not agree to this, the friars' second request was that the missions, at least those that belonged to the Colegio de Querétaro, be transferred to a more secure area. The viceroy acceded to the latter idea; the three missions that belonged to the college at Querétaro were approved for transfer. The three missions that were administered by the college at Zacatecas remained in the east until 1773.

In 1730, at least one of the three Queretaran missions was placed along the Colorado River in present-day Austin, Texas. No one is exactly sure of the location, but some archaeologists have suggested the area around Barton Creek. However, this settlement did not take because the friars found the area "unacceptable." The San Antonio region was growing rapidly with Spanish, Native Americans and Anglos, and the abundant water supply allowed for, and enticed, further immigration. The area was becoming a hub for the entire territory; the mobile missions were soon headed there.

The first Mission Concepción in the San Antonio territory was erected in the spring of 1731 along the eastern banks of the San Antonio River, approximately one league south of Mission Valero and equidistant north of Mission San José. According to Burke, "It was erected on the site where the 'lost mission' of San Francisco Xavier stood before it was moved to join Valero to become one of the four missions which the Alamo, in its checkered history, absorbed."[64]

The new Mission Concepción acquired a somewhat different name after being reestablished. At this new location, it was renamed Nuestra Señora de la Purísima Concepción de Acuña. This added cognomen was another honorific for the new viceroy of Nueva España, Juan de Acuña, Marqués de Casafuerte.

The three new missions in the San Antonio area were initially constructed, as missions had been in the east, of wood stakes and slats, thatched roofs and some adobe. Still, the new mission suffered the usual troubles at the beginning. There were constant, seemingly ubiquitous Apache raids against the people and deprivations on the cattle and horses. There was little food available for the residents, so a "loan" had to be given from the stalwart Mission San Juan Bautista. According to Habig, Concepción required the delivery of 1,280 bushels of corn and 250 head of cattle. But this was debt not long in its repayment, since the Franciscans, the few soldiers allotted to them and the natives all strove to cultivate the fields necessary for the next

Sketch of Concepción, nineteenth century. *Courtesy of Witte Museum, San Antonio, Texas.*

year's crops and even began the construction of the acequia with which to irrigate the land. The latter job was so well completed that the acequia still exists and provides water to the immediate area.

After seventeen years, the wooden structures were gradually replaced with stone and mortar, and the mission began to materialize into what we see today. Father Fernández de Santa Ana, who succeeded Father Vergara (Father Hidalgo's successor) as the primary religious figure at Concepción, was the man who began this extraordinary building. A stone wall was constructed encircling the entire compound, which comprised quarters for the neophytes and a few soldiers; a convento for the religious; and the requisite rooms for textile, metal, masonry and food preparation. The church, a cruciform structure, was built with a nave measuring approximately ninety feet by twenty-two feet. Soon after, the dome was added and the twin bell towers erected. As mentioned earlier, if Mission Valero had ever been fully completed, it would have greatly resembled the edifice of Concepción, save the third tier planned at Valero. As Quirarte noted, "Inside the front entrance of the church was a well-built vestibule made of painted and varnished wood. It had two inner doors with an iron bar. The floor was made of carefully laid brick. The door of the baptistry had an iron grating and a latticed window. The choir loft, with a vaulted ceiling, had a railing made of turned wood."[65] Of the interior of the church, Habig states:

On the altar in the church there was a carved statue of Mary Immaculate; and in the sacristy, on a smaller scale, a life-size statue of Our Lady of Sorrows, and also a large crucifix. In the church was one confessional and one bench—no pews. Two large carved, cedar chests in the sacristy contained the vestments and sacred vessels. Everything needed for divine service was on hand.[66]

In the summer of 1745, Father Francisco Xavier Ortiz was sent by the college at Querétaro to inspect the missions in Texas; he spent just over a month in San Antonio and made much comment on the progress at Concepción. He noted that the walls of the church were forty-five inches thick, with rock enclosing the adobe both inside and outside. Ortiz also saw that, even though there were Indian quarters made of adobe within the surrounding walls, there were still some neophytes living in wooden huts, or *jacales* (*xacales*), within the perimeter. At that time, the mission housed roughly 250 Indians of various tribes.

Mission Concepción. *Image courtesy of author.*

Of the façade, Ortiz wrote that the main niche over the portal door was for the statue of Our Lady of the Immaculate Conception. And on either side of the main door, the moon and sun were painted—another attempt by the friars to conjoin the two religious philosophies, their own and that of the neophytes. Others have written that these two images, the sun and moon, are meant to represent the crucifixion, the moment of Christ's death, when former sins (the moon) pass away and a fresh beginning (the sun) is offered. Over the doorway, the mission's artist added the following inscription:

A SU PATRONA, Y PRINCESSA
CON ESTAS ARMAS, ATIENDE
ESTA MISSION, Y DEFIENDE
EL PUNTO DE SU PUREZA

The translation states: "For its Patron and Princess, with these arms, this mission serves [Her], and defends the expression of Her purity." The rope entwined around this inscription is a symbol for the Franciscan Order, as are, in part, the "MAR" and "AVE" (Ave María) on the shield. Even though the façade is "beautiful," the masonry work around the portal is less ornate than at San José. The addition of the Romanesque half columns, or pilasters, on either side of the main door, though, does contribute a grand expression to the entrance. And, as at San José, when finished, the entire façade of the church was painted with a polychrome, geometric design—a similar pattern as those on the vigas in the ceiling at Mission Socorro.

Because Concepción was closer to San Antonio than the other four missions outside of town, it enjoyed slightly more success with the natives than did its sister missions. A report proffered to Father Ortiz (who was, by 1762, the custos of the college at Querétaro) illustrates that the church and its environs were completed and that the crops and neighboring rancheria were flourishing. The report lists several groups of Native Americans congregating at the mission, chief among these the Sanipao, Pajala and Tacone, all of them Coahuiltecans. However, these three were by no means the only groups represented at the mission. In fact, so many different Native American dialects were spoken at the mission that Father Gabriel de Vergara, who had been a friend and colleague of Espinosa during their time in east Texas, wrote a dictionary of sorts of the different tongues. This work centered on the Pajala dialect, since it was the dominant one spoken. Unfortunately, like Sappho's poems, only a fragment of this work exists today. Indeed, the Pajala dialect was used so extensively at the mission that the acequia was called "Pajalache Ditch."

The first three decades of Mission Concepción's presence in the San Antonio area were fruitful. Not only did the Franciscans have an adequate number of natives to help work the land, but the land, well taken care of, was taking care of its residents. Even though another epidemic swept through the mission in 1739 (probably measles and smallpox), again cutting the population in half, the number of natives willing to try this European experiment steadily increased over the next twenty-five years. The natives within the mission also enjoyed the benefit of self-governance, with a few being elected to run their own affairs within and around the mission. But tensions were already smoldering between the natives, the missionaries and the residents at San Fernando and at the Presidio San Antonio de Valero. The mostly Canary Islanders residing at San Fernando, and also those migrating toward those missions to the south, had been made to believe that, as in New Mexico, the neophytes were at their disposal for manual labor, a misconception that the Franciscans repeatedly tried to correct. Of course, this intercession by the Franciscans on behalf of their charges only further irritated the Spanish, who, as a whole, felt entitled to whatever resources the land might offer. Furious letters were written back and forth by settlers and Franciscans alike to the governor, who frequently sided with the Spanish settlers, much to the dismay of the missionaries.

The report delivered to Father Ortiz in 1762 listed 58 Indian families within the mission's walls. Counting the unmarried, the total number of persons was 207. However, the numbers continued to decline from this point forward. Habig writes that one reason was that "the missionaries were unable to make extended trips for the purpose of bringing back runaways and adding new converts, because a military escort was not provided for them."[67] By 1771, the Franciscan in charge down the river at Mission San Juan Capistrano was experiencing even more reductions in neophytes than was Concepción. His plan had been to travel to La Bahía and convince as many Native Americans as he was able that life nearer the Presidio San Antonio was better than life where they were. Habig notes that 107 were willing to join those missions farther up the San Antonio River and were distributed among the four missions. Concepción received 16, 10 of whom had left Mission Rosario, only adding to the problems that mission was already facing.

The second reason given for the overall population decline at Concepción was de Croix's order of 1789 making all unbranded cattle government

Altar, Mission Concepción. *Image courtesy of author.*

property. It cannot be overstated how much the missions depended on these herds and how injurious was the half-peso tax. The constant Apache depravations, the killing and/or stealing of the beeves by Indians and local residents and finally de Croix's decree all but ensured for the missions that their primary food source and, indeed, the one aspect that attracted the most neophytes was removed. By the end of that same year, in what Habig terms the "last detailed report" from Concepción, a Father Joseph Francisco López writes, "Concepción had only seventy-one mission Indians." A beef shortage, though, could not have been the sole reason for the decline in numbers of neophytes for the brothers. The abuses by the Spanish settlers and soldiers, together with the relative safety and comfort of the San Fernando area, were also causes for the decrease.

As with the entire mission effort in Nueva España, sooner than later the Spanish government grew tired of the constant expense and troubles at the missions. As mentioned earlier, Mission San Antonio de Valero was secularized in 1793; Concepción was soon to go the same way. One year later, the other four missions south of Valero were "partially secularized." Pedro Huízar was appointed alcalde of Concepción and began the minutiae of itemizing the materials and surveying the land around the missions. Once he had completed this work, the next step was to distribute all the land and animals among the natives.

The Franciscan missionaries remained at their posts for the next few decades, administering to the spiritual needs of the remaining population. But Huízar was tasked with the daily maintenance of the compound. Father José María Camarena is listed as the last resident minister of Concepción. He, along with Governor Manuel Múñoz, assembled the Indians to inform them that "they would now receive farms of their own which they would have to cultivate to provide for their needs, without the missionary's supervision."[68] Records from this year indicate that there were approximately forty Native Americans living at the mission. Soon thereafter, Father Camarena left, and the missionary at San José assumed the ecclesiastical responsibilities for both missions.

Ceiling fresco, sun image at Mission Concepción. *Image courtesy of author.*

By 1797, the population at Mission Concepción had been reduced to such a number that the captain of Presidio Nuestra Señora de Loreto at La Bahía asked Governor Múñoz if he could have the bells from the "abandoned" Concepción, since the two at his presidio were cracked. It appears that after Huízar had doled out the surrounding lands to the natives, there were few residents within the mission's walls. Indeed, by 1809 the census reports only twenty Indians but thirty-two Spaniards. The other issue with secularization was that some of the natives, once told that the routine of the missions as they had come to view it was to cease, returned to their former groups.

The early nineteenth century was, as has been mentioned, a very tumultuous period in Spanish colonial Texas, due in no small part to Napoleon's invasion of Spain and Portugal. The wars on the Iberian peninsula were causing the Spanish government to fracture, and the esteem of the church in Spain was disparaged. The troubles and concerns of a colony thousands of miles away certainly seemed more trivial than securing the homeland and driving Napoleon out. In such an environment, many men in Mexico saw an opportunity to withdraw from Spanish domination and invent their own histories.

Priest-turned-soldier Miguel Hidalgo y Costilla, the "Father of Mexican Independence," began, in 1810, one of the first attempts at independence from Spain. Hidalgo's venture failed, but it spawned others. The revolt the next year of Juan Bautista de las Casas ended with Casas's head displayed on a pike in San Antonio. However, the seed of independence had been planted, and in quick time it flourished. Troops under one Bernard Gutiérrez de Lara found some success in 1813 when, in an effort to lay siege to San Fernando and the presidio of San Antonio de Béxar, they occupied Concepción. Their advance resulted in the surrender of the San Antonio complex, but only for a time. Gutiérrez resigned his office as president of the new provisional government later that year and left for New Orleans, there to continue his martial efforts for some time. At the same time, however, the Spanish had reclaimed the San Antonio region.

While nearly void of residents, Mission Concepción continued to breathe, although with shallow, labored effort. Those who did still live at the mission were now taking their religious instruction and services at San José. Concepción limped along for a few more years until final and formal secularization occurred on February 29, 1824. As Habig observed, "Thus Mission Concepcion, which had merely lingered for an entire decade, finally died. Its existence as an Indian mission came to an end."[69] Nevertheless, people continued to live within and around the mission. The aqueduct was still in use, and those natives who had been granted land in the area took advantage of the resources. Meanwhile, the idea of independence from the ruling authority had also been nourished. Now, even the Anglo immigrants grew desirous of self-governance.

In October 1835, still another battle for independence took place near Mission Concepción. Ninety Texians under the leadership of Colonel James

Bowie and Captain J.W. Fannin took over Concepción as their base of operations. On October 28, they were surrounded by over four hundred Mexican troops. The truth of the matter is that the battle was fought just behind the mission at a bend in the river. As far as the mission is concerned, the Texians used its towers as lookout posts, although some sources mention that parts of the mission's grounds were damaged in the fighting. Ignoring orders from Stephen Austin to return to the larger contingent of the army, Bowie and Fannin waited for the Mexican army and caught them in a crossfire. The long rifles of the Texians were deadly accurate, and the Mexican troops were repulsed as far as San Antonio. As Burke wrote, "Here, at Mission Concepción, the Texans had won their first fight with the Mexican troops."[70]

After this encounter, the mission was granted a significant rest from activity. For the next few decades it lay dormant, with only the local residents wandering through its now overgrown grounds and crumbling walls. Of course, as with any vacant building from the past, the locals routinely helped themselves to the rock and adobe of the structure to build their own homes and fences. In 1850, the traveler John Russell Bartlett came upon Mission Concepción, just as he had at San José. The narrative of his wanderings, published in 1856, gives a wonderful insight into the condition of the entire area as well as the mission:

> *The two towers and dome of the church make quite an imposing appearance when seen from a distance, but, on approaching it, we found it not only desolated but desecrated; the church portion being used as an inclosure for cattle, the filth from which covered the floor to the depth of a foot or more. Myriads of bats flitted about, which chattered and screamed at our invasion of their territory; and we found nothing of interest within the church to repay us for encountering their disagreeable presence.*[71]

Just before Bartlett's adventure through the region, the newly founded Republic of Texas had traded the title of the mission and surrounding land to the Catholic Church, with Bishop J.M. Odin receiving formal possession in 1841. Odin, in turn, allowed the Marianists (Brothers of Mary) under Andrew Edel to use the property. Edel founded St. Mary's Institute, later to become St. Mary's University. The Marianists at least cleaned the church and prevented it from fading into obscurity, ostensibly sometime after Bartlett's visit. In 1911, this Society of Mary returned title of the lands to the bishop of San Antonio. Very soon afterward, the Sisters of Charity of the Incarnate Word opened an orphanage called, at that time, St. Peter's–

Original crucifixion fresco at Mission Concepción. *Image courtesy of author.*

St. Joseph's Home. Today, that same institution (now affectionally called St. PJ's) exists just across from the mission on Mission Road.

Only a few years later, in 1919, St. John's Seminary was established next to Concepción. (The archdiocesan website, however, states that both the orphanage and the seminary were founded nearly simultaneously in 1929, when the Franciscans returned.) It still stands today and is easily seen just behind and to the northeast of the mission as one faces the façade. There is even a Margil Hall, commemorating Father Antonio Margil de Jesús, founder of both the College of Nuestra Señora de Guadalupe de Zacatecas and Mission San José. St. John's has undergone much renovation and restoration itself in the past seventy-five years. It is proudly owned by the Diocese of San Antonio and continues to educate those choosing to enter into this special vocation.

In the 1930s, as it did with the missions in Texas and so many other locations around the country, the WPA undertook some minor renovations to Concepción; walls were shored, and some minor roof repairs were accomplished. In the 1970s, archaeological work was begun, and much of Concepción's original premises were discovered, including some of the original rooms for smithing and textiles and even some of the Indians' rooms. After this work was completed and the mission was added to the state's historical sites list, the mission had a couple of decades of quietude. The complex was maintained by the Archdiocese of San Antonio for a number of years, until 2008, when Father David Garcia was asked to continue the "ministry" of restoring the region's other four missions. Mission Concepción, being first along the river just south of San Antonio, became the first to receive Father Garcia's attention.

Today, the Archdiocese of San Antonio owns and is responsible for only a relatively small portion of the area at the missions. As Father Garcia recently commented, "We [the Diocese] are only responsible for the church buildings themselves, where we celebrate Mass. Originally, the Archdiocese owned everything and it was becoming a huge burden to keep it all going."[72] And so it reached an agreement, a "partnership," with the National Park Service (NPS). The archdiocese owns and maintains the church, interior and exterior, while the NPS is responsible for everything else connected to the mission.

As for the restoration work itself, many different organizations have had a hand in the effort. For one, the Texas Society of Architects (TSA) has accomplished much of the primary restoration. An essay written by Rebecca Roberts for the organization's website describes how some of the more intricate work was carried out:

> *The interior restoration of Mission Concepcion required the removal and replacement of crumbling plaster. Although the structure was originally built*

Ceiling molding detailing original artwork. *Image courtesy of author.*

during the 1730s and 1740s, the contemporary mission walls incorporate more-recent plaster from repairs done in the 19th and 20th centuries.... [The] plan was to remove any loose plaster and replace it with a lime-based plaster replicating the historic 19th-century plaster. However, as they began to work, they made an interesting discovery; the remnants of Spanish frescoes on the original wall beneath the 19th-century plaster.[73]

When completing this work, the TSA took considerable pains to remain true to the original efforts of the Franciscans, who, along with the invaluable assistance of their Native American neophytes, had constructed such an incredible edifice where nothing but woods and grasslands had existed before. Roberts concludes: "The discovery of the original frescoes was fundamental to the overall restoration of Mission Concepción. When the interior was repainted at the conclusion of the project, the hues were mixed to match the pigments of the unearthed frescoes."

Indeed, all of this work has produced the most remarkable effect. Not only does Concepción appear today much as it did nearly 250 years ago, but as reward for everyone's attention to the mission's purpose, Mission Nuestra Señora de la Purísima Concepción was also included as a UNESCO World Heritage Site in 2015.

MISSION SAN JUAN CAPISTRANO

In July 1716, Father Isidro Felix de Espinosa founded Mission San José de los Nazonis in east Texas. The Nazoni, it will be remembered, were a part of the Tejas group whom the Franciscans were trying to instruct. The mission, like all those in the area at the time, was abandoned in 1719 due, again, to the threat of a French invasion. The mission was reestablished as part of the Aguayo expedition of 1721, with Father Espinosa returning to his duties in the region. Less than a decade later, for reasons already stated (mainly fiscal), this mission, as with Concepción, was moved to an area at or near present-day Austin. Because conditions proved too inconvenient along the Colorado River, or perhaps because the burgeoning San Antonio area appeared more inviting, the mission was moved again, to the spot where it now stands: approximately four leagues from the heart of the city, San Fernando Cathedral. When finally settled, on the east side of the river, the mission was renamed San Juan Capistrano (Saint John of Capistrano, the "soldier-saint"). The renaming of this mission has led to some speculation. What was the reason for the change? Some suggest that Mission San José y San Miguel was already sufficiently established and that there was no need for another of a similar name. Others have written that John of Capistrano had been canonized only a few years prior, so his name was on many of the Franciscans' minds. But even this latter argument is difficult to sustain, since Capistrano was "canonized" twice: once in 1690 by Pope Alexander VIII, and again in 1724 by Pope Benedict XIII. That his name should have been offered at all is an issue for the reader.

Of the mission's location, some think that the spot was preordained when Terán and Father Massanet traveled through the territory in 1691 on their way to the eastern portion of the state. Both Terán and Massanet kept journals of their wanderings, and both mention a flat, woodless plain very near what would later be named the San Antonio River. (It should be remembered that Massanet was the individual who named the entire region for San Antonio de Padua on this trip.) As Habig writes, "The 'level lands without woods' which they crossed when they continued their journey would then have been the flying fields of Brooks Air Force Base."[74] It is of course almost impossible to know for sure if this was the area mentioned by Massanet, since the landscape and the river's course certainly would have changed over several decades.

As with the other missions in the San Antonio region, San Juan Capistrano was established at a predetermined distance from San José in order to keep the peace between the different factions of the Coahuitecan Indians. At first San Juan catered to the same Pajalats as at San José. However, the inclusion of other groups such as the Pcana, Camasugua and Tacame ensured that the missionaries' work was consumed not only with trying to acquaint the Indians with the semi-enclosed, European lifestyle but also with keeping the infighting to a minimum.

The building of the mission, too, was arduous work. As with all of the missions, San Juan was initially constructed of wood walls and thatched roofs. Of the more permanent construction of the buildings, Jacinto Quirarte, with usual succinctness, states:

> *The church was made of brush plastered with mud and roofed with straw and had a tower with two bells. A stone church was finished by 1756. The construction of a larger church was begun sometime after 1777, but the building ceased in 1787 because there were not enough laborers available and building materials were scarce.*[75]

Whatever stage of progress or state of readiness the mission attained, it was, like all of the missions and even the Villa of Béxar itself, under frequent Apache and Comanche attack. Mary Maverick, in her memoir, writes often of Comanche raids within San Antonio. The missionaries at the missions wrote very often of Apache raids on their cattle, horses and anyone who ventured outside the protection of the mission's walls. As James Burke noted, "San Juan Capistrano did not make as much progress as the other San Antonio missions. Its exposed location brought it under frequent Indian attacks, and the lands allotted to the mission were not sufficient for its horses and cattle and the raising of the required crops."[76] Indeed, even the mission's proximity to the river did not guarantee that the waters would reach the fields. The missionaries and the Indians had to dam up the river and divert its flow just in order to irrigate a small portion of the area. But the physical location of the new mission was not the only concern.

As with the other missions, the epidemic of 1739 severely decreased the natives' numbers and resolve. Next, as had happened before, the Indians

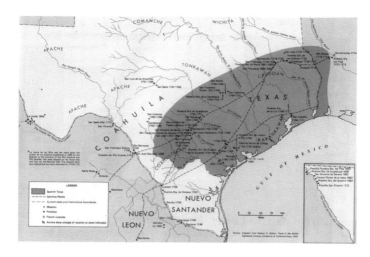

Map of Coahuila and Texas. *Courtesy of tshaonline.org.*

noticed that the Franciscans were not getting along with their own. One man in particular became as much a hindrance to the mission's progress as the Apache raids.

Carlos Benites Franquis de Lugo was governor of Texas for almost exactly one year, from 1736 to 1737. Franquis had been sent to Texas to help administer the province, since the presiding governor, Manuel de Sandoval, was not residing at the provincial capital of Los Adaes in the east. Rather, he was busy with Apache raids in central Texas and was primarily residing at Presidio San Fernando de Béxar. For this seeming lack of attention, Franquis had Sandoval arrested. However, the trouble seems to have been born not from mismanagement by Sandoval but rather by the pernicious mentality of Franquis himself. As Robert Weddle wrote of the despot, "Franquis, of violent nature, set immediately upon a stormy course which assured his name of a place in history but won him also the enmity of almost every missionary and presidial official from Saltillo to Los Adaes."[77] The man was evidently deranged; Weddle again notes that Franquis "made himself obnoxious to all by claiming that the presidios of Coahuila, as well as those of Texas, owed him the same obedience due the Viceroy or the King."[78] If the toxic nature of the new governor had been the only thing the missionaries had to contend with, the Spanish might have enjoyed a little more success. But the arrogance of Franquis knew little boundary.

After arresting and dismissing Sandoval, Franquis implemented one strategy that ensured failure for most every mission and their charges: he decreased the number of soldiers at San Juan and, indeed, at all the missions from three to one. Franquis seemed indifferent to the fact that these soldiers had been instrumental in helping the friars with the missions' construction and maintenance, that they were responsible for keeping the Apache far from the missions' walls and that they were directly responsible for retrieving runaway neophytes. The disastrous results were evident soon enough. Habig noted that the most deleterious effect of the soldiers' removal was the impression it had on the Native Americans already gathered at the mission:

> *Encouraged by the disrespectful attitude of the governor toward the missionaries, some of the Indians felt quite safe in disregarding the padre's directions and violating the rules of mission life. Some of those at San Juan Capistrano joined others of Mission Concepción in making false depositions before the governor concerning alleged mistreatment by the missionaries.*
>
> *Actually, as some of the witnesses testified later, it was the governor himself who had the depositions prepared; and the Indians and others were told that they must sign them. When Lieutenant Mateo Pérez firmly objected that the accusations were not true, the governor threatened to banish him from the Province of Texas, "farther than any place he could imagine," if he did not add his signature.*[79]

Pérez did become a dupe of Franquis, as is evident from later records. In such an environment there can be no respect for rule, and the natives soon and simply left the mission. And without the requisite number of soldiers on hand, there was no one to reach into the woods to try and retrieve them. The reports from the end of that year list about twenty Thelojas and only a few Orejones Indians still at the mission. As for Franquis, even though his term as governor of the province was mercifully short, his psychosis enjoyed a long life.

The delusions of Franquis spread all the way down to the Mission San Juan Bautista. He demanded to know why his orders to remove the soldiers had not been carried out at the mission along the Rio Grande, too. Father Miguel Sevillano de Paredes, of San Juan Bautista, responded that only the viceroy could issue such orders and that if it was true that Franquis had removed solders from their posts in the San Antonio area, then he, Sevillano, would have need to write about the matter to the viceroy. Of course, Franquis's malfunctioning temperament could not sustain rebuke. He began searching the messengers relaying mail between San Antonio and San Juan Bautista. When the friars heard of this, they began to hide their correspondences under the saddles of those delivering the mail. Finally, in

1737, a letter from Sevillano, his *Consulta Apologética*, arrived to the viceroy. The letter detailed the governor's abuses and neuroses. The outcome was exactly what one might imagine:

> *The result* [of the letter] *was a new enjoinder to Franquis that he should improve his relationship with the missionaries and restore the soldiers to guard the missions, under penalty of suspension. The Governor refused, however, and his removal from office was ordered under date of July 11, 1737. He was instructed to retire to San Juan Bautista while the resident judge, Fernández de Jáuregui, investigated his official report.*
>
> *...The deposed governor turned the trip into a ludicrous affair by his repeated scoffing at the missionaries in general and Father Sevillano in particular. All the religious, he asserted, were but missionaries of Satan.*[80]

Within a year, Franquis was awaiting his trial and the soldiers had been resupplied to the missions. The new priest at San Juan Capistrano was Father Mariano Francisco de los Dolores y Viana. And, in fact, it was Father Mariano who had dealt with Governor Franquis while the latter was in the San Antonio area. But still another scourge awaited the mission even after the lunatic governor had been replaced.

Only a little more than a year had passed when another smallpox epidemic raged through the region in 1739. Some have written that the friars themselves helped to spread the contagion as they traveled between missions trying to help the sick. Nevertheless, the records from the time report that at San Juan Capistrano, in the year 1739, the approximately 220 Indians at the mission were diminished to a paltry 65. Many of these succumbed to disease, while others ran away from the mission and, in the natives' minds, its inherent evils.

During the course of the next couple of years, the missionaries, with the aid of the Spanish soldiers, were able to re-congregate several of the Indians who had returned to their previous habits. Even though Mission San Juan Buatista had to succor its sister mission with basic supplies, the reports of Father Francisco Xavier Ortiz, one of 1745 and another of 1756, reveal that San Juan Capistrano was reinvigorated by, if nothing else, a lack of catastrophe. Ortiz, in his first report, notes that the irrigation ditch was supplying the fields handily and that the year's crops were "sufficient" for those at the mission. Also, in his official report, Ortiz records that the ecclesiastical work had been progressing through storm and darkness. Over 500 natives had been baptized since 1731, and just over 200 had received last rites before their deaths. The same year's report lists "a total of 163 persons, of whom 113 were baptized Christians and 50 were catechumens."

Ortiz's report of 1756 details an increase in almost every aspect of mission life. The crops were producing, and the ranch was stocked with several hundred head of cattle and sheep. Additionally, the buildings of the mission were now made of stone and mortar, and the church contained the necessary ancillary items with which to perform the sacraments. Habig writes:

> *A church, with a sacristy, had been built of stone and mortar. It was a long narrow building 24 varas (about 80 feet) long, and 5⅔ varas (about 19 feet) wide. Its roof consisted of good beams of hewn wood. There was also a good granary, which was a stone building.*[81]

The façade of San Juan Capistrano is most unusual when compared to the Missions Valero, Concepción and San José. Instead of the Romanesque belfries, Capistrano has a single front wall adorned with a trinity of bells above the portal doors; the top bell (the third bell, evidently) was a later addition. The church and nave are very simply one long cruciform shape, with the transepts nearer the front door being quite short. The singular

Façade of Mission San Juan, 2007. *Image courtesy of author.*

aspect of the building suggests a unity of purpose, but it is impossible today to know whether the architect had any such notion in mind. Of course, the mission contained the usual convento, Indian quarters and multiple rooms for storage and workshops.

Even though Capistrano contained all the requisite equipment and personnel for a mission, Father Morfi, during his inspection tour of 1778–83, reported that Capistrano was only adequate and did not compare with Concepción or San José. Critical as this seems, it is still not difficult, even today, to understand why Father Morfi may have had a rather myopic view of Capistrano. The mission does still seem remote from the other missions, and one does experience a sort of isolation when visiting. To imagine the area 250 years ago, without the roads and surrounding homes and buildings, is to envision the desolation of those first missions in the east.

As mentioned earlier, at Concepción in 1771 the effort of Captain Luis Antonio Menchaca to bring natives from the coastal regions to the San Antonio area resulted in an additional 107 neophytes for the Franciscans. Of that number, 65 were placed at Capistrano. For the next couple of years, the mission carried on as well as could be expected. When the Spanish government expelled the Jesuits in 1773, the missionaries from the college of Querétaro were asked to replace their Jesuit brothers in California, Arizona and northern Mexico. At that time, the Franciscans from the college at Zacatecas took formal control of those missions in Texas. The next report from Mission Capistrano described, in some detail, the mission's structures and inhabitants. Father José Francisco Lopez wrote to the Spanish government that Capistrano had 58 neophytes, categorizing them by married couples, bachelors, children, widows and widowers. Lopez's report also mentioned that of these natives, the majority were of the Marahuitos group but included the Pamaques and Orejones.

The secularization decree of 1794 mandated that Pedro Huízar again be employed to survey the mission's grounds and property. At this time, there were only thirty-six Indians residing at the mission. Huízar divided the land into plats for each family and then subsequently meted out the utensils, animals and equipment among the same. The records from this period indicate that the Apache raids and the tax on the unbranded cattle had taken a severe toll on the provisions. Within the next dozen years, Mission Capistrano became a "sub-mission" of Mission San Francisco de la Espada, with the resident missionary traveling between both to administer sacraments. As a mission unto itself, Capistrano saw its end soon enough.

In 1823 the government of independent Mexico decreed their full and complete secularization; and the following year Father Diaz de Leon surrendered the church of San Juan Capistrano and its furnishings to the acting pastor of San Fernando. Thus the mission finally ceased to exist.[82]

As with all the missions in the San Antonio region, the nineteenth century was a time of upheaval followed by scant attention. Quirarte mentions that "the roof blown off by the hurricane in 1886 was replaced by 1907."[83] Travelers such as Bartlett, Roemer and Kendall all took notes on the mission's fragile nature. When one wrote of crumbling walls, another would note that the floor inside the church was broken up for grave sites. It was in the 1830s, during the Texas bid for independence, that Antonio de Padua María Severino López de Santa Anna y Pérez de Lebrón, or simply General Santa Anna, entered the area. Besides the notoriety (or infamy to some) that the general gained at Mission Valero, López de Santa Anna also left his mark at San Fernando. It was from this vantage point that he gave the signal to attack the Alamo and to leave no prisoners. Mission Capistrano, relatively distant as it was, also could not escape the dictator's attentions. According to Burke:

It was in this chapel, one account has it, that the Mexican president and dictator, Santa Anna, "married" the child he renamed Leota a dozen days before the battle of the Alamo. His sharp and amorous eyes fell upon her as he rode in to the town with his troops, and that night he had her brought to his quarters to make her his mistress.[84]

As one may imagine, there has been much speculation as to the truth of this event. Some sources say that "Leota" was Melchora Iniega Barrera, the seventeen-year-old daughter of one of the families living around the old mission. The account states that she remained with the dictator for several days but was sent back to Mexico before Santa Anna's defeat at San Jacinto. It is not difficult to imagine that the tale is valid when considering that Santa Anna's other two marriages were to women under the age of twenty.

For the next several decades, Mission Capistrano suffered from the neglect attendant to its abandonment. This mission and San Francisco de la Espada owe much of their present state of preservation to Francis Bouchu. Bouchu was a Frenchman who arrived in Texas in his late twenties and was ordained as a Catholic priest in 1855 at Galveston. At first assigned to minister at San Fernando, Bouchu was later assigned to the churches at Espada and

Mission San Juan, 2016, after reconstruction. *Image courtesy of author.*

Capistrano. Although residing primarily at Espada (he is credited with restoring much of that mission by himself), Bouchu took an active interest in Capistrano. According to Escobedo, Bouchu "restored the church and a postcolonial house in the compound and rebuilt portions of the old walls."[85] Sadly, when Bouchu passed away in 1907, the mission's renovations ceased, as well. Aside from some reconstruction done to the chapel by the Sons of the Immaculate Heart of Mary in the early twentieth century, no further work was undertaken until the WPA, in the 1930s, discovered portions of the original site other than the church itself. Other work to the walls and church interior was begun in the 1960s.

While Habig was writing his text on the San Antonio missions, archaeological work had just begun at Capistrano. At that time, the church, convento and structures attached to the church were rebuilt. With the recent archaeological surveys in hand, Habig wrote:

> It was planned indeed to build a larger and better church on the east side; and when there was still a large number of Indians at the mission, in the 1760's no doubt, the building was begun. But after one half of the structure was completed, the project had to be abandoned because of the lack of Indians in the mission. The ruins of this half-completed church can still be seen on the west side. It was never used as a place of worship.[86]

After several more years of minor restoration efforts, the mission was added to the Register of Historic Places in 1972. Since that time, the four missions along the San Antonio River have been placed in several different joint custodianships—partnerships between the church and entities such as the Texas Parks and Wildlife Department and the National Park Service. Nine years ago, this writer wrote an article on these same missions. At that time, Capistrano had not undergone the restoration it enjoys today. The exterior walls were still gray and weathered. Also, and very sadly, the doors of this church were padlocked then. The sign on the door gave the reason for the lock: some theft had occurred, and since there was no permanent employee to watch over the facility, the church had had no choice but to bar entrance. Later, it was learned that in August 2000, three wooden statues dating to the colonial period had been stolen from the altar. Happily, since the restoration, theft is no longer an issue, although the three statues remain lost.

The most recent work to the mission has just been completed, mainly through the efforts of the archdiocese via the stewardship of Father David Garcia and the several architectural and renovation teams he employed. As

Interior and altar of Mission San Juan. *Image courtesy of author.*

for the work at Capistrano, Father Garcia stated that the mission was in a very fragile state when his work began. He said, "We did a major stabilization of San Juan because it was actually in danger of falling. So, we had to go under the church putting piers and beams and things to make it stable."[87] In fact, it was while this work under the church was going on that the workers discovered more than they had anticipated. As Father Garcia recounted:

> *In front of the door of the church we found fifteen sets of human remains from the Colonial Period. We had to stop work in that area because there's a protocol you have to follow from the Texas Historical Commission; you have to pay for archaeologists to come and see what else they might find. That's just a reality of working with old church buildings, because cemeteries are right inside the front door usually.*

When asked what became of these "remains," Father Garcia said:

> *In this case, we buried them on the other side of the compound. The local Native American group was involved in the ceremony to do that. The remains had to be verified by the archaeologists at UTSA [University of Texas at San Antonio] who gave them over to me and I gave them over to the Native American group who held a ceremony that lasted for days.*[88]

As a final word, Father Garcia stated that he, along with the several groups who assisted him in all of this reconstruction and restoration, is most proud that, in 2015, Mission San Juan Capistrano was listed as a UNESCO World Heritage Site. A visitor to the site will certainly experience that pride.

Mission San Francisco de la Espada

With the exception of Mission Valero, all of the missions along the San Antonio River had their beginnings in east Texas. San Francisco de la Espada is no different.

As mentioned before, the de León entrada of 1690 produced Mission San Francisco de los Tejas in eastern Texas for the Nabedache tribe of the Tejas group of American Indians. It was the zealous Father Massanet who had been employed to lead the religious portion of this entrada. After establishing the mission and finding the local Indian population agreeable

Mission Espada, unrestored. *Courtesy of Library of Congress.*

as potential conversos, Massanet and de León returned to Coahuila to ask permission to erect a string of missions along the eastern border. The viceroy, Gaspar Conde de Galve, assigned Don Domingo Terán de los Rios, Texas's first governor, to lead the group back to the east. For his part, Massanet brought along nine Franciscan priests and a few *donados* (acolytes) to undertake this enterprise. One of those chosen to assist was none other than the indefatigable Father Francisco Hidalgo.

The Terán entrada was also responsible for the establishment of the complex that would become La Bahía, initially along the coast as a means of receiving support from the sea. In addition, during the absence of Massanet and Terán, Father Casañas, relatively alone in the wilderness of east Texas, had established Mission Santísimo Nombre de María just on the east side of the Neches River. Such an incredible exertion of will as Father Casañas demonstrated in that time, by himself, is a testament to the faith and determination of some of these priests. So, when Massanet and Terán returned to the eastern missions in 1691, they found evidence of some progress but also much more misery than they could have anticipated. An epidemic (smallpox, measles or some other contagion) decimated the local population in 1690–91, claiming not only thousands of Native Americans but also some of the Spanish religious. The situation was so desperate that when Terán left to return to Coahuila in January 1692, six of the missionaries decided to return with the group. Indeed, the meager and infrequent resupplying of these early missions in the east did little to stave off the inevitable decline and abandonment. As Espinosa reported in his *Cronica* concerning the Terán-Massanet entrada:

Having entered in 1692, at the beginning of February, the governor left for that distant land [la tierra afuera, i.e., Coahuila] with his group; and in this group were some of the religious who had made the entrada with him. [These religious left] *because the unpleasant events from so costly a journey had made them lose their spirit and they hoped to return to the quietude of their convents. With the absence of the governor and soldiers, the hopes [estimaciones] which the Indians had had at the beginning, were deflated to a large degree. So, of the fifteen soldiers* [remaining], *some died, others deserted, and of the nine who stayed, they considered themselves alone and at liberty [solos y libertados] and were not considering that they should conduct themselves in the manner of a Christian, many times neglecting their responsibilities to the Indians.*[89]

It has already been mentioned that the departure of Terán from east Texas caused friction between himself and Massanet when the governor had requested, and been denied, much of the mission's supplies for his return trip. By most accounts this could be viewed as the first clash within the Texas territory between the Franciscans and the Spanish government, the first conflict of philosophy within the mission system: whether the purpose was to convert Native Americans or simply to subjugate and claim the land. If an answer lies in this particular instance, one should remember that Terán's party left with all that they requested because, very simply, they took it.

The difficulties experienced by those who chose to stay among the Tejas tribes for the next two years can only be imagined. The missionaries were largely ignored by their own government, and the military presence was more of a nuisance than an assistance. So, when the missions in the east were ordered abandoned and Massanet had buried the bells and cannons and burned the mission, the inhabitants retreated for Coahuila, with four of the few soldiers who had stayed deserting along the way. By the time they reached Monclova, Father Massanet was so exhausted in body and mind that he retired to the college at Querétaro, never to cross the Rio Grande border again. Father Casañas became a missionary to the New Mexican missions, where he was martyred in 1696. And Father Hidalgo, never wavering in his conviction of the potential religious successes that waited in the woods of east Texas, was instrumental in the Domingo Ramón entrada of 1716–17.

The Ramón expedition, as mentioned earlier, established six missions in, basically, the same region in the east where the prior efforts had been made. It was this entrada that included Father Isidro Félix de Espinosa, the custos

Altar at Mission de la Espada. *Image courtesy of author.*

of the Colegio de Querétaro, and also Father Antonio Margil, custos of the Colegio de Zacatecas. With so distinguished a group, the first mission constructed in the east was named Mission Nuestro Padre San Francisco de los Tejas. This mission was founded in July 1716 about three leagues farther east of the other mission in the vicinity and was to cater to the spiritual needs of the Nacona and Cacachau tribes of the Tejas group. It was built on the west side of the Neches River, near today's Bowle's Creek, which meanders between Rusk and Cherokee Counties.

Even though the government had provided a presidio this time, the troubles that Father Espinosa writes about during his own tenure in the east are difficult to imagine. The problems were such that, when the French "invasion" of 1719 occurred, eventually all of the Spanish in the east departed for the relative security of San Antonio to await the arrival and support of the Marqués de Aguayo.

Much has already been described about how the Aguayo entrada, being well supplied and informed, was unusually successful. Missions and presidios were established in east Texas, and those at La Bahía would finally take their

Mission Espada, nineteenth century. *Courtesy of Witte Museum, San Antonio, Texas.*

permanency. The San Francisco Mission in the east acquired a new name, San Francisco de los Neches. The diarist Father Juan Antonio de la Peña describes the early achievements of the Franciscans in rich detail.

Even though Father Espinosa had been successful in getting the natives to agree to remain at the missions and develop a sort of permanent, or pueblo, lifestyle, the agreement was short-lived. As Marion Habig wrote:

> *The Indians were probably sincere in their promises at the time of Aguayo's visit, but they were fickle and did not keep them. They failed to settle down around the Mission San Francisco and the other re-established missions. And as far as supplies for the missions were concerned, the missionaries were confronted with the same problems as before.*[90]

The irony is that, due to the Indians' passivity, the inspector of 1729, Pedro de Rivera y Villalon, decided to close Nuestra Señora de los Dolores de los Tejas Presidio. With that action, the Franciscans from the college at Querétaro decided to close their mission in the east and take themselves to the San Antonio area. When they left, those Franciscans from the college at Zacatecas remained for several more years, catering to the religious needs of the Native Americans, for whom those three expeditions had been conducted.

So it was that Mission San Francisco de los Neches was transferred to the San Antonio River area—albeit only those items that were mobile or able to be carried hundreds of miles, quite literally by foot. There the population was being daily augmented by Indians, English, Spanish, French and Russians. After finding a suitable site at least one league away from the other missions already established in the region, the Franciscans now founded Mission San Francisco de la Espada (Saint Francis of the Sword).

Almost as much has been written about the name of this mission as about its history. It seems no one is entirely certain from where the cognomen "Espada" derives. Burke writes that the title is associated directly with St. Francis, who, while experiencing a vision,

> *saw himself in a splendid apartment filled with all kinds of arms, rich jewels, and beautiful garments marked with the sign of the cross. In the midst of them stood Christ, who said, "These are the riches reserved for my servants, and the weapons wherewith I arm those who fight in my cause." From this Saint Francis thought that he was to be a great soldier, and it is from this phase of his life that Mission San Francisco de la Espada received its militant name.* [91]

While this is a very romantic and awesome explanation, Burke does overlook the fact that, before St. Francis was a "saint," he was, in fact, a soldier—and a very good one. Habig contests that the nomenclative addition is akin to those like "de Valero," "de Acuña" or "de Aguayo." However, his assertion is not based on a specific individual, only that Espada "was in use as a Spanish surname." To support this assertion, Habig mentions that a captain at Presidio Nuestra Señora de Loreta de la Bahía was named Manuel de Espadas.

To further his claim, Habig also contends that the addition of "Espada" has nothing to do with the architecture of the church's façade; such a theory was evidently circulating at the time of his writing.

> *Espada could not have derived its name from the shape of the belfry of its chapel, which some have thought resembles the hilt of a sword; for, it was called "de la Espada" before the chapel was built or even planned. Until the 1740s the Espada Mission had only temporary structures.* [92]

Whatever the origin of the honorific "Espada," it would not be a leap of faith to imagine that those priests, living as rough a life as they were and remembering their founder's martial beginnings, might adopt a cognomen that reflected the duty, sacrifice, strength and perseverance of a dedicated and stalwart soldier.

Crucifix at Mission Espada. *Image courtesy of Angie Browne.*

Mission San Francisco de la Espada was about three leagues, or nine miles, from the San Fernando church and Mission Valero—both considered the center of San Antonio at the time. Even today, when one visits all four of the missions in a single trip, it is very easy to realize just how distant, exposed and threatened the mission must have been. The records indicate that the Apaches raided Espada with more frequency than they did the other missions, and when other troubles befell the missions (the 1739 epidemic, for example), it was Espada that suffered the most, simply because it was the most remote. In this way, Mission Rosario at Goliad and Espada endured similar fortunes. The records of the friars and writings of several authors mention that the Native Americans who congregated at Espada were, in the early to mid-eighteenth century, safe within the mission's walls but, once outside, were easy prey for the Apaches. Many of the stories are very unpleasant to read, much less to relate. Nevertheless, the Apaches were by no means the only trouble that the mission faced.

In 1736, Mission Espada was in the care of Father Pedro Ignacio Ysasmendi. That same year was the term of Franquis de Lugo as governor of the province. Habig notes, "He [Ysasmendi] was singled out by Governor Franquis de Lugo as a special target upon whom he vented his meanness."[93] Mention has already been made of Lugo's madness, and the result of his (the governor's) behavior and edicts served to countermand the friars' authority at the missions. For this most-removed of missions, that lack of authority and respect increased with each successive mile from San Fernando. By the spring of 1737, the natives, their attitudes and beliefs already wavering, began to leave the mission to return to the woods. When Father Ysasmendi asked for a few soldiers to help search for the Indians, the governor refused. Next, when those neophytes remaining within the mission's walls saw how nothing was done to help retrieve these who had run off, they, too, took to heel. Habig notes that the custos of the college of Querétaro was residing at Mission Concepción at this time. It was to him that Father Ysasmendi wrote asking for help. The "Father President" responded that, per orders of Lugo, he could do nothing.

> On June 8, Fr. Ysasmendi wrote to Fr. President that all the other Indians of Mission San Francisco had followed the example of the Tacames on the day before and had gone off to live in the woods. Of the 230 Indians who had been at Espada, all of them Christians, not a single one remained.[94]

After Lugo's removal from office and a few attempts to reclaim the "Christian" Indians who had left the mission, Father Ysasmendi reported in late 1737 that 108 neophytes had returned to live at the mission. But the joy was to be brief, as the epidemic of 1739 destroyed the routine and lives of everyone living along the San Antonio River. Records indicate that, at the time, Espada had approximately 120 Native Americans living either within or near the mission's walls. By the time the calamity had passed, only 50 remained. Among those who perished during this horror was none other than Father Ysasmendi. This wound healed slightly with the 1771 expedition of Captain Menchaca, who delivered 26 neophytes to Espada from the coastal region.

During the next few decades, Espada prospered, as did the other missions in the region. Crops flourished because the acequia was maintained properly, irrigating the fields for the entire San Antonio mission system. The reports of Father Ortiz, both in 1745 and 1756, indicate that steady progress was being made at the mission. His 1756 report relates that the stone-and-mortar church he had seen begun in 1745 was completed. Ortiz noted that the nave, or interior, was cruciform and approximately thirty-six varas long and fourteen varas wide. Unfortunately, as Jacinto Quirarte mentions, "The Espada church was rebuilt several times. The sacristy was used as a temporary chapel during all those periods of construction."[95] These intervening years were still prosperous for the mission. The small

Acequia (aqueduct) for Mission Espada and surrounding lands. *Image courtesy of author.*

chapel contained two altars, the convento was two stories and contained four rooms upstairs and three downstairs and the granary was made of stone and mortar, as were the walls and other main buildings. Of the Indian housing, Father Ortiz mentions that in 1756 their stone housing was still under construction and many were living in stone-and-mud jacales along the riparian area just outside the mission walls. Within eight years, the stone apartments had been completed, and most of the mission natives lived inside the compound. Habig reports, "The number of Indian families living in the mission in 1762 was fifty-two, and the total number of persons was 207. For its defence [sic] the mission had two swivel guns and sixteen firearms with a supply of ammunition."[96]

For approximately thirty years, the missionaries in charge at Espada attempted to expand the mission by constructing a larger chapel in which to hold services. These efforts appear to have been sustained even after the missionaries from Querétaro were made to occupy the Jesuit missions in the Sonoran Desert, turning their charges over to the missionaries of the college of Zacatecas. From the 1730s to the 1770s, each successive missionary tried to erect a new chapel. However, as has been written, all of these attempts failed due to lack of resources.

Sometime before 1777, at the end of which Fr. Morfi visited the San Antonio area with Teodoro de Croix, the church which had been in the process of construction at Mission San Francisco for a long time seems to have been completed; but it was poorly built and had to be torn down because it was in danger of collapsing.[97]

Morfi described the entire complex as "ill-arranged and plain." Conversely, he did mention that the mission was accomplishing its work by listing the Mariquitas and Pacaos among the Native American tribes gathered there; in total, Morfi wrote that 133 persons were living at Espada during his visit.

As with all the other missions in the region, Espada was partially secularized in 1794. Once again, Pedro Huízar was given the task of surveying the land and taking inventory of all the supplies, tools and animals at the mission. These were divided up among the Indians who were living at the mission.

According to the records kept at the time, from 1813 forward, there was but a single priest in charge of the four missions outside of San Antonio proper. Father Bernardino Vallejo was in charge of rites and sacraments at both San José and Espada for a few years. By 1820, Father Anzar, from La Bahía, was called over to perform the last rites for a resident at Espada.

The final Franciscan in charge of the four missions along the San Antonio River was Father José Antonio Díaz de León. Father Díaz was priest when, in 1824, the final secularization of the mission was completed. It was he who signed the final inventory lists and delivered these to the priest at San Fernando. Following this, the mission soon began its ultimate decline. "During the years that followed the secularization of the mission, though people continued to live there, the church was completely neglected."[98] The most notable aspect of this era is the fact that, sadly, the few people who chose to live near the mission were constantly attacked by hostile Indians. The next major historical event comes in October 1835, when Bowie and Fannin, along with about one hundred men, occupied Espada and repulsed a Mexican force twice their size. This would at least suggest that the mission's walls and chapel were still standing at the time. In the same year, according to Burke, the notorious outlaw Sam Bass camped at Espada, where, as one of his many Texas hideouts, he hid much of the loot of his robberies.

A little over twenty years later, the resolute Father Bouchu took a special interest in the mission and, just as at San Juan, spent much of his time and energy rebuilding what the years had wasted away.

With his own hands he rebuilt the side walls on the old foundations, and then plastered and whitewashed them. He put a tin roof on the chapel, and placed doors at the entrances. Inside the chapel he laid a wooden floor, built a choir loft, set up a sanctuary railing, and installed simple but sturdy pews. There were still some old statues on hand of St. Francis, the Blessed Virgin, and the Christ Crucified. These he regilded and put on the altar in the sanctuary.[99]

Father Bouchu lived at Espada for the remainder of his life, caring for this mission as well as San Juan. He kept meticulous records of all the catechisms, marriages and baptisms he performed in the area. He also wrote a catechism for children, in Spanish, which was, at first, printed by himself and then reprinted for many years after. Bouchu died in San Antonio in 1907. Without his efforts, it is quite possible we might have lost this extraordinary edifice.

In 1911, yet more restoration was undertaken, and a new ceiling and roof were built. The old floor was replaced with brick, and the church was once again open for Mass by 1915. During the same year, a school was opened at the mission and run by the Sisters of the Incarnate Word. This school served the community until 1967.

Façade of Mission de la Espada, 2016. *Image courtesy of author.*

When restoration work began on the other three missions along the San Antonio River, Mission Espada was not excluded. The archaeological, restoration and renovation teams that Father Garcia organized beginning in 2008 gave Espada the same attention to detail that the others received. Quirarte, however, maintains that "the only original part of the church is the front wall or the façade. Father Bouchu added all the other walls during the years from 1858 to 1907."[100] Still, with the doorway's Moorish design and the wonderful two-tiered belfry, it is something of a miracle that, if only one portion of the mission was to survive, it was to be this. The icon of St. Francis, which adorns the main altar, is thought to also be from the same time period and to be the very one Father Bouchu repaired when he lived at the mission over a century ago.

Today, just as with the other three missions along the "Spanish Missions Trail," Espada is an active community Catholic church with a regular Mass schedule. It was included as a part of the UNESCO sites in 2015.

The four missions of the San Antonio Missions Trail are, in a word, extraordinary. Their creations, journeys, histories and subsequent revitalizations tell a tale not often available in this country; our history is still a relatively new one. That is not to intimate that the work is completed; it is only the period in which we find ourselves. The final word on these four incredible churches belongs to Father Garcia:

> *It's a never-ending job, because these buildings are so old you always have to be looking at what's the next project. I mean, just because you've done a restoration doesn't mean you can come back twenty-five years from now; you have to be on top of it constantly.*[101]

CHAPTER 5

THE MISSIONS AND PRESIDIOS OF SAN XAVIER, SAN SABÁ AND EL CAÑON

I n the eighteenth century, Apachería described an area of land extending from just below the Llano Estacado region of Texas through New Mexico and into Arizona. Within the boundaries of what would become Texas, this territory ranged from just about Balmorhea in the west, stretching toward the San Antonio area in the east, touching on the Big Bend region to the south and terminating in the northwest at Comancheria, where the Comanche and Taovayas tribes roamed. Today's I-10 freeway would have bisected this enormous tract.

As has been mentioned, when the Spanish were first making their mark in east Texas, almost all of the Native American tribes in the Texas territory were inimical toward the Apache, and vice versa. Most notably, within the limited scope of this book, the Apache tribes continually harassed Spanish settlers, soldiers and religious alike because of their association with those Indians who had been hostile to the Apaches for generations. Additionally, those natives who had resolved to stay within the Franciscans' missions were made frequent targets of the bellicose Apaches. As the San Antonio area grew and the Camino Real's ruts became deeper and more obvious, the Apache issue had to be addressed. For the Spanish government, the answer was simple: hunt them down and kill or make slaves of them all. Such a militaristic solution was anathema to the Franciscans. Their desire and plan was precisely the opposite; the friars wanted to pacify and convert the Lipan Apaches by placing missions within their territory. In this way, so the priests believed, all the native tribes would learn to coexist. And, as usual, these two

SPANISH MISSIONS OF TEXAS

contradictory philosophies were going to proceed while conjoined but then become mutually undone. The friars' philosophy, by its nature, was unable to exist with that of the government.

In May 1745, Native Americans of the Tonkawa group (Mayeye, Yadosa and Yojuanes) approached Father Mariano Francisco de los Dolores y Viana, one of the priests in charge of Mission Valero in San Antonio, to establish a new mission in their area just to the northeast of San Antonio along today's San Gabriel River, then called the San Xavier River. Father Dolores, in cooperation with the other priest at San Anton de Valero, Fray Benito Fernandez de Santa Ana, undertook to satisfy these wishes. The Indians had already selected a site for the priests. A few months later, Father Dolores, accompanied by a Querétaran colleague and visitor to the territory, Father Francisco Xavier Ortiz, met with the Tonkawa group and discussed the potential project. Father Dolores was particularly enticed by the expedition and agreed to ask for formal permission from the government for the necessary supplies. It was Father Dolores who stayed with the neophytes while Ortiz returned to make the proposal to his superiors at Querétaro.

The authorities at the college readily agreed to the project, mainly because the Indians had already congregated at a site.[102] Then began the long wait for official approval from Mexico City, wherefrom the requisite money and personnel would need to stream. Some officials argued against the venture, claiming the land was infertile and too exposed to Apache attacks. Fray Dolores wasted no time, however. While waiting for the "official" proclamation, he built a temporary mission named Nuestra Señora de los Dolores del Río de San Xavier. The Indians had asked and waited for this effort for so long that Father Dolores soon found himself not only exceedingly successful in his duties but, in fact, overextended. As Herbert Bolton notes:

> *Indeed there were more Indians than could be supported, in spite of the supplies which Fray Mariano [Dolores] had brought; and before the end of March he was constrained to tell the neophytes not to solicit any more tribes, to refuse food to all of those already there except such as were actually helping in the fields and at the missions, and to send word to the tribes on the way to remain at a convenient distance.*[103]

Even though it was two years in coming, the project was approved. However, as Weddle points out, the authorities had other interests as a result of their decision: "The Indians gathered in the San Xavier missions had to be won away from the French, who had established trade relations with them. And, being enemies of the Apaches, they had to be protected from them."[104] Ultimately, the viceroy, Francisco de Güemes y Horcasitas, Conde de Revilla Gigedo, gave his blessing to the project and approved the construction of three missions along the river, near present-day Rockdale, Texas, to be attended by two religious each from the college at Querétaro. Mission San Francisco Xavier de Horcasitas was formally established in May 1748. Nine months later, Mission San Ildefonso was erected in February 1749 for this same Indian group. As sources indicate, it was very close to Mission Xavier. Father Juan José Ganzábal was placed in charge of this second mission. At San Ildefonso, numbers of the Coco tribe assembled. With members of their confederate Tonkawan tribes already residing at both missions, a third mission was erected two months later, Mission Nuestra Señora de la Candelaria.

At first, with all three missions so close together (literally in a line approximately one league distant from each other along the south bank, with a smaller tributary running behind) and all administering to the same Native American group, things progressed as the missionaries and natives had hoped.

With the missions prospering, officials began deliberations on how best to manage and protect their interests. As was expected, the government initially considered placing a presidio somewhere near the three missions. Father Ortiz, already experiencing trouble with the thirty soldiers assigned to the missions, suggested that a community of settlers be encouraged instead. Having visited Mission San Antonio de Valero for some time, he had seen the success that immigration could have on the neophytes, advocating a domestic rather than militaristic hand. Nevertheless, the college at Querétaro requested, and was granted, a presidio for its endeavors. Ironically, when the decision was made (after years of quarrelsome wrangling and dickering) to construct a new presidio for the San Xavier missions, it would be this work—to protect and serve the missionaries and the Indians—that would desecrate the missions and their purpose.

Presidio de San Xavier de Gigedo was authorized in 1751. Captain Felipe de Rábago y Terán was given command of the complex and its garrison of fifty soldiers. At the beginning, the soldiers were allowed to have their families with them. Later, when frequent Apache attacks weakened the resolve of many of the compound's members, the families were sent back to San Antonio. This served only to poison the already festering animosities between the religious and the military. The soldiers complained that now there was no one who might prepare their meals after a hard day's work and that their wives were no longer around to clean their apartments within the missions and at the presidio. The sexual aspect of the wives' absence should not go without mentioning, and it was this final complaint that led to wanton, prurient and licentious behavior. The soldiers, with their commander's enthusiastic approval, grabbed, groped and raped the natives' wives and daughters. If the male Indians complained, they were usually beaten, imprisoned or both. But it was not only the Native Americans who were violated by the soldiers.

At the time Presidio Gigedo was founded, the San Xavier missions had progressed, with relative success, for two years. Indians and missionaries alike had been eager to construct a lasting relationship; it was, for the briefest of moments, a uniquely beneficial situation for both parties. History has demonstrated, though, that human relationships grow more intense and volatile as the groups' numbers are augmented by singular members. Even though the Coco, Deadose and Mayeye tribes were willing to allow the Franciscans to bring their life's work to fulfillment, the Spanish *solados* were frequently composed not of regular, disciplined soldiers but the remnants of the outlying presidios and settlements. Of the original thirty soldiers who came to the San Xavier missions, many could be referred to as such only because they wore uniforms. And, as is constantly reaffirmed, when responsibility is given rather than earned, that responsibility is soon abused. When the presidio was constructed and the fifty men under Captain Rábago came to the San Gabriel area, the relationship for all concerned was forever changed for the worse.

To complicate matters for the Franciscans, the governor of Texas and Coahuila at the time, Pedro de Barrio Junco y Espriella, had been, from the outset, opposed to missions in the San Gabriel region. When commanded by Viceroy Gigedo to visit the area and scout for a suitable location for a presidio, he recommended consolidation of all three missions into a single compound, to be transferred to the San Marcos River basin. As such, the missionaries found their work hindered, once again, by those from whom they should have drawn the greatest support. And, once again, the neophytes were witness to the infighting between those in whom they had placed their trust and safety. This situation, coupled with the daily abuses at the hands of the soldiers, caused many of the neophytes to abandon the missions. The decline in numbers only strengthened Governor Barrio's opinion that these missions were not sufficiently peopled to warrant further supply. In truth, the tolling of the bell had sounded as soon as Captain Rábago was given his command. One incident, which started while Rábago was recruiting soldiers in San Antonio for the San Xavier Presidio, would ruin Fathers Dolores's and Ortiz's work at San Xavier.

Captain Rábago disliked his assignment from the beginning. While still in San Antonio recruiting soldiers for the new garrison, Rábago had seduced the wife of Juan José Ceballos. The cuckolded husband learned of the affair while en route to the mission's complex. Ceballos complained to the captain, who reproached the soldier for daring to insult a superior and had him arrested. Once at Presidio Gigedo, Ceballos was placed in the stockade.

Spanish colonial flag, Cross of Burgundy. *Image courtesy of author.*

The friar in charge of Mission Candelaria, Father Miguel Pinilla, was also the priest for the church at the presidio. (It should be recalled that the families of the soldiers were at this time living at the presidio's and the missions' compound. Ceballos's wife was certainly there, too.) Father Pinilla, after learning of the situation, asked and then demanded that the captain cease the affair and release the soldier. Father Pinilla was rebuffed and mocked.

At some point, Ceballos escaped from the presidio jail and made his way, for sanctuary, within the walls of Mission Candelaria. While Father Pinilla tried to work out a resolution, Captain Rábago only became enraged. He made every attempt to have Father Pinilla removed as priest of the presidio. In turn, the missionaries wrote their letters to the college at Querétaro asking for help or even to have the presidio removed. There seemed no other way to deal with the hostility of the military. As Weddle commented:

> *Father Dolores himself, who had been the moving spirit in the founding of the missions and the presidio, now asked the Viceroy to have the San Xavier Presidio removed, preferring to risk the depredations of hostile Indians rather than the excesses of the licentious Captain.*[105]

The situation only worsened. Rábago began encouraging his subordinates to bring him women from among the Indian population. Still, those Indians who had remained watched in disbelief as their tutors and protectors argued among themselves, all the while suffering the atrocities and indignities committed by the soldiers. The religious could see no expedient way out of this intractable situation. When Father Pinilla heard of still another adulterous affair between an officer and an enlisted man's wife while hearing confession, he had had enough. Fray Pinilla instructed Father Juan José de Ganzábal, who was presiding priest at San Ildefonso Mission, to deliver a message to the presidio. The note announced that, due to all of the soldiers' sins, he, Father Pinilla, as head of the missions at San Xavier, was excommunicating everyone at the garrison. Weddle writes, "Most of the soldiers soon were penitent, however, and within a short time, all were granted absolution."[106] Even though this act of charity could have cleansed the infection of insubordination, events to follow made certain that no such healing would ever occur.

On May 1, 1752, the members of the Coco Nation, disillusioned, abused and bewildered by all they had endured and witnessed, abandoned Mission Candelaria en masse. The religious, no longer able to rely on the military to help retrieve the fleeing natives, allowed themselves a few days of respite while trying to sort through their limited options. It was a week and a half after the exodus of the Coco, while Fathers Pinilla and Ganzábal were having dinner with Juan José Ceballos at Mission Candelaria, where the soldier had found sanctuary, that a gunshot through a window felled Ceballos. Father Ganzábal ran to the door to try to see or catch the assassin, but he, too, was shot in the heart—his death the result not of a gunshot but of an Indian's arrow.[107]

In a few days, an Indian of the Sayopín tribe named Andrés arrived at Mission San Juan in San Antonio. Toribio de Urrutia, captain of the Presidio San Antonio de Béxar, had Andrés arrested, and he soon confessed to shooting the missionary; his payment for the deed was a horse. Andrés also told how the entire ordeal had been the concoction of some of the soldiers at the Presidio Gigedo under the guidance of Captain Rábago. Sources state that Andrés soon recanted but that Urrutia did not believe it. He investigated and implicated Rábago in both murders. The captain was stripped of his command and spent eight years in a cell in Mexico (probably at Mission San Juan Bautista) while his case was attended.

Even though the guilty had been dealt with, spirits at the missions of San Xavier continued to wither. Smallpox again spread among the missions, and a long drought began to dry the river into stagnant ponds. The remaining Indians retreated to their old haunts. Indeed, as if a curse lay across the area, the commander chosen to replace and indict Captain Rábago, Captain Miguel de la Garza Falcón, fell victim to the epidemic.

It is a paradox that the conciliation of the troubles at the San Xavier missions should have come in the form of a close family member of the one who had done his best to eradicate the missions. After the death of Captain de la Garza, his successor was none other than Don Pedro de Rábago y Terán, the uncle of Felipe. Don Pedro's arrival had taken three years, but his plan, while perhaps not totally rescuing Father Dolores's ideal, at least extended its intent. Against viceregal orders, Don Pedro de Rábago y Terán ordered the missions and presidio along the San Xavier River moved to the San Marcos River, near present-day San Marcos, Texas, in 1755. The reasons for this relocation were both to try to stop the hemorrhaging of the missions at San Xavier and to support the long-standing plan to incorporate a Spanish missionary presence among the Apache Indians, with whom so many had experienced trouble over the previous eighty years. In addition to the San Marcos River area, the Llano and San Sabá Rivers had also been scouted for the same purpose. Indeed, Father Santa Ana had been a proponent of just such a move for some time—to settle the Apaches onto missions along the San Sabá within Apachería. Of course, the reasons for doing so, as mentioned earlier, were obvious: to mollify and convert the Apaches would be to finally pacify the entire territory. However, what the Spanish could not understand was that their dealings with the Apaches would signal betrayal to all those for whom they had just spent years, effort and supplies trying to convert. "The friend of my enemy is also my enemy," the saying goes. And when Don Pedro de Rábago y Terán died in 1756 at San Marcos of still another epidemic, those friars who had long dreamed of a settlement along the San Sabá now had their opportunity.

Because the San Sabá effort was to cater to the Apaches, those natives of the Tonkawan tribes who still remained hopeful and faithful at San Xavier were asked to make the trek to the missions of San Antonio so that their ecclesiastical needs could be cared for there. McCaleb writes that the church ornaments, bells, vestments and other sacred items also were to be removed to San Antonio.[108] A few decades later, some of these items were transferred to the new Mission Nuestra Señora del Refugio, which would be the last mission established in Texas and run by the college at Zacatecas.

Due to the slow machinations of the Spanish colonial government, plans to relocate missions to the San Sabá region were long in developing. Even though more than one thousand Apaches had come to the missions at San Marcos,[109] the despair of the place could not support the idealism of the Spanish, and the Apaches were put off. Only Fray de los Dolores, who had always dreamed of a mission along the Guadalupe River, stayed behind while the others retreated, once again, to San Antonio to await instruction, supply and reassurance. Father de los Dolores's mission, San Francisco Xavier de Horcasitas, was re-founded ten leagues from San Antonio on the Guadalupe River near New Braunfels. This mission, the reincarnation of the first at San Xavier, would last for about two years, closing in March 1758 when those at San Sabá were finally realized. Some have mistakenly named this Mission Nuestra Señora de Guadalupe. That mission, however, was in Mexico, near the confluence of the Rio Conchos and Rio Grande, La Junta de los Rios.

William Dunn, writing a little over a century ago, stated:

> *The mountainous region north of San Antonio traversed by the Pedernales, Llano, and San Sabá Rivers had long been considered a suitable locality in which to found missions for the Apaches. It was the favorite dwelling place of these Indians, since its ruggedness afforded numerous strongholds against the hostile Northern tribes, and to its refuge the Apaches usually fled after one of their extended raids. Nowhere did they feel as secure as in their familiar haunts along the San Sabá.*[110]

Of course, this region is a large portion of Apachería. And it was this territory that the Spanish viceroy Conde de Revilla Gigedo was surveying for the new Lipan missions. Father Hidalgo had seen this land a few decades prior and had gained the same impression. At the time, it seemed, the only detractor to the idea was the governor of Texas, Jacinto de Barrios y Jáuregui. Governor Barrios considered the Apaches' overtures insincere based on their recent, pugnacious past. As Weddle writes, "In the mind of the Governor, the Apaches merely wanted the protection of Spanish arms against the hostile Comanches, and therein lay the danger."[111] While many of the governor's opponents, the Franciscans among them, thought his suspicions narrow-minded, history can only laud his prescience.

There exists, in the scant records from the time, evidence that the French tried to stall the Spanish advance into Apachería for some time with claims that the area was already staked by them. This gesture was shrugged away by the junta convened to discuss the matter of the missions and subsequent presidio. This group approved a garrison of one hundred soldiers; most of the quarreling within the junta owed to the complaint from some quarters that several of these men were to be taken from the presidio at Béxar. This argument was fundamentally belied by the supposed truth that, in the event of the Franciscans' success with the Apaches, the armed forces guarding

San Antonio would become redundant. And, with this obstacle overcome, the way forward for the San Sabá Missions was paved. The region's new viceroy, Agustin Ahumada y Villalón, Marqués de las Amarillas, proffered the formal decree in May 1756, appointing Colonel Diego Ortiz Parrilla commander of the new presidio.

Colonel Ortiz was given much of the responsibility associated with this newest mission effort. His tasks included transferring the property of the San Xavier missions to San Sabá and building not only his presidio but also three missions. Before any of this was undertaken, he was instructed to assemble the fifty soldiers from San Xavier and another twenty-two from San Antonio's presidio and recruit an additional twenty-seven "of good moral character."

While the labors of the military and of construction fell to Ortiz, the religious matters fell to Father Alonso Giraldo de Terreros. Father de Terreros had served the crown with as much distinction as had Colonel Ortiz. Born in Spain, he had taken his orders in Mexico at the age of just twenty-two. Only two years before this venture, Father de Torreros had established Mission San Lorenzo in Coahuila, Mexico, certainly one of the main reasons for his appointment. Another reason for Father de Torreros's appointment was that his cousin Don Pedro Romero de Terreros, a wealthy mine owner, had

Presidio San Sabá, front gate. *Image courtesy of author.*

promised the viceroy that he would underwrite the expedition into San Sabá if his cousin Alonso was placed in charge of the missions. The government, duly noted, duly complied. The terms stipulated that Don Pedro's financial support was for three years, that his power was only ecclesiastical in nature (the government would carry the tab for the military) and, lastly, that the religious needed to be taken from the college at Querétaro and the Colegio de San Fernando de Méjico, which had been organized a couple of decades before in 1734.

Colonel Ortiz and Father Terreros, after proceeding from Mexico into Texas, met at the usual juncture: Mission San Juan Bautista. The colonel had gathered his twenty-seven soldiers, and Ortiz had assembled his group. Among Father Terreros's group were two missionaries from the college at Querétaro and two more from the college of San Fernando, one of whom was Father José de Santiesteban Aberín. Also with Father Terreros were several families of Indians from Saltillo who would, as had become customary, act as ancillary tutors for the Franciscans in their work converting the neophytes.

The two groups met at San Antonio and waited out the winter of 1756. During this time, Father Dolores, still attending to the second Mission San Francisco Xavier de Horcasitas, asked that his mission be included in Pedro Terreros's generosity. Father Terreros explained that such a fiscal decision was not his to make. The refusal served only to anger Father Dolores, who had tried for so long to work among the Apaches. Colonel Ortiz, who had had misgivings about the Apaches and the new missions from the start, now had a religious confederate. In tandem, these two openly opposed the San Sabá missions even before they were constructed. Indeed, Father Dolores so resented Fray Terreros that he took a *mozo* (a young acolyte) who had been sent along from Mexico to attend to the priest and then refused to store the supplies for the San Sabá missions at Mission Valero. He instead insisted they had to be kept a few miles away at Concepción.[112] As was the case in many of the mission compounds, the matter of whose authority was greater, the religious or the military, became yet another reason for the failure of the entire enterprise. But the one element that seemed sure, at least to Father Terreros, to cause failure was Colonel Ortiz's constant delaying. However, it must be remembered that it was winter. While the Franciscans were ready to move, the soldiers were not. There was also the matter of the huge numbers of cattle and sheep that needed to be transported from the coast to San Sabá. If these were brought north in the middle of winter, several would not survive the journey. It was Father Terreros's contention, on the other hand, that by stalling through late winter, they would miss the time for planting the crops, and this would ensure both that there were none the next year and that some of Don Pedro's funds would be wasted. Further, when the cattle and sheep did arrive at San Antonio, Colonel Ortiz pastured them along the San Marcos River; he had decided that there was not ample room for them where they were. In fact, by early spring, after the train had left San Antonio, almost all the supplies were being held at San Marcos, guarded by a contingent of soldiers.

Terreros was further frustrated when Colonel Ortiz took a circuitous route from the San Marcos River, back through San Antonio and meandering for over a week before reaching the San Sabá area in April. After reaching the proposed spot, Ortiz officially proclaimed the region unfit for settlement. He pointed out that, unlike what the Apaches had promised before, they were not gathered at the river to meet them; in fact, there was not an Indian in sight. The priests countered that if the military did not fulfill its obligations and orders to do what was necessary for the religious's efforts, they would return to Mexico and file formal complaints. Ortiz was persuaded to stay.

It was decided to construct the presidio a league farther down the river so as to lessen the threat of the soldiers' interfering with the neophytes' instruction. The mission was to be on the river's south shore, the presidio on the north. As Weddle observed, "While this placement reduced the likelihood of military meddling in mission affairs, it rendered impossible defense of the Mission in case of attack."[113]

The mission was constructed in the usual manner, made from the available wood and straw or grass. A chapel was built, as were quarters for the religious, the Tlaxcalteca families that accompanied the friars and the awaited neophytes. All the necessary rooms and buildings were erected within a strong, wooden outer defensive wall. (It is argued by some that this site was almost exactly where Mission San Clemente had been constructed in 1684.) An irrigation ditch was begun, and the crops were finally planted. (Dunn wrote in 1914 that the ditch could still be evidenced along the river.) Even though plans had called for two missions—one for the priests of Querétaro and the other for those from San Fernando—only the Querétaran mission was constructed, since there were, literally, no Indians at the site. And so Mission Santa Cruz de San Sabá had its beginnings.

At the same time, Colonel Ortiz busied himself with erecting his garrison. He also built a tall, defensive outer wall and, inside, wattle-and-daub rooms for his soldiers, officers and their families. The presidio, as was customary, also included a chapel for the soldiers, where one of the mission's priests

Interior of San Sabá. *Image courtesy of author.*

would come regularly to offer Mass, hear confession and administer the other holy sacraments. The garrison was given the name Presidio San Luis de las Amarillas.

Throughout the early summer, no Indians—Apaches or otherwise—came to the mission. Father Terreros was becoming frustrated, and Colonel Ortiz was ready to pack it in. Terreros sent Father Benito Varela, who knew the Apache language, to scout for them. Varela went to the soldiers still guarding the rest of the supplies at the San Marcos River and asked whether they had had any contact with the Apaches. The priest was told that an Apache woman·had related how her group had been attacked along the Colorado River by a confederacy of Tejas and Comanche Indians and that they all had to scatter or be killed. It was disheartening news, and the friars did not have long to wait before the Apaches made contact near San Sabá.

By the middle of June, a few thousand Apaches did arrive near the San Sabá River. The Franciscans were delighted; one can only guess the reaction of Ortiz and his garrison. The priests invited the Apaches, whom they suspected were the neophytes who had promised to organize at the missions over a year before, to join them inside the compound. The Franciscans were disappointed to hear the Indians' claims that they were merely passing through the region on their way to hunt both buffalo and those northern tribes who had so recently attacked them. The priests were crestfallen, but Ortiz was not surprised. A seasoned Indian fighter and experienced soldier, Ortiz had been expecting just this sort of behavior. H.H. Bancroft, writing just over a century later, held the same opinion:

> *Missionary influence, so potent a factor in the advance up to this point, was utterly powerless against these brutal rovers; treaties were of no avail, for they were never kept by the Indians except so long as it seemed for their interests to keep them, as a means of putting the Spaniards off their guard in preparation for renewed hostilities; extermination was the only remedy, a slow operation not yet fully carried out after more than a century of effort.*[114]

At this point, even Father Terreros was becoming exasperated. He continually wrote to his cousin Pedro, expressing his private pain and doubts. Even his most trusted colleague, Father Francisco de la Santísima Trinidad, who had been the mission's most ardent supporter after Terreros, was losing hope. When the same group of Apaches returned several days later, again the missionaries' hopes were hoisted. The spiritual celebration was short-lived, though. The Apaches told the friars that they were only passing through on their way back south. According to Weddle, the Indians seemed anxious and expectant. They left the area too soon and even then left little that could have been taken as a sign of their return to settle at the mission. Fathers Terreros and Trinidad both wrote letters to the viceroy stating that they believed they had failed but would remain at the mission until formally recalled. Colonel Ortiz had also written the viceroy, asking permission to vacate San Sabá. His troops and strength could be better used to the north, at the Los Adlmagres Mine. His request was rebuffed, and the colonel was reminded of his responsibilities toward the religious and their purpose.

After the Apache group had left, most of the Spanish began to doubt the reason for staying. Not only were there no souls to convert and save, but the fact that only one mission was erected was clear evidence that the whole enterprise might very well be an enormous mistake. It was time for someone to make a decision, to take action.

> *Yet it was the Queretaran missionaries who asked permission to return to Mexico, leaving two of those of San Fernando to look after the mission with*

Father Terreros. Thoroughly frustrated, the missionaries felt the uselessness
of their presence here. The new mission afforded them no opportunity
whatever to serve. Some of them felt it would be better to return to Mexico
immediately, rather than to continue the fruitless effort.[115]

Father Varela, who had gone in search of the Apaches, was first to leave. Next, the two missionaries from the college of San Fernando began to give support to those aspirations they had kept contained for so long; they, too, wanted out. In their letter to the president of their college, they wrote, "We find no reason why we should remain with this enterprise, which we consider ill-conceived and without foundation from the beginning."[116]

Permission was granted, and these two also vacated the mission before summer was out. By early autumn, only two Franciscans remained at the mission, Father Terreros and Father Santiesteban, one from each of the two colleges. Fray Trinidad, in January 1758, was sent to Mexico with letters for the government and the two colleges. For whatever reason, one more missionary arrived just after Trinidad's departure. Father Miguel de Molina arrived in early February 1758 from the college of San Fernando. The contingent of religious, less the Indian families that had accompanied Terreros, made up the population at the mission. The presidio, on the other hand, was much more active, since the soldiers and their families were still maintained there. Dunn surmises that there were "probably three or four hundred persons at the presidio, two hundred and thirty-seven of these being women and children."[117]

Besides those mentioned, the only Native Americans who visited the mission were small groups of Apaches on their way south to cross the Rio Grande. They each told the same story. A very large group composed of Indians from the northern regions, Norteños, were gathering to exact their revenge on the Apaches. The later months of 1757 passed with only rumors of this attack. Then, beginning in February 1758, the rumors grew into action. In late February, a group of Indians stampeded the horses of the presidio during the night. Alarmed by this, Colonel Ortiz ordered six soldiers to ride and warn the expected supply train of potential hostile Indians in the area. These six were attacked along the way, and the report brought back to Ortiz made him certain that the rumors were true. Ortiz, the experienced Indian fighter, tried to advise Terreros:

Parrilla repeatedly urged the padres to forsake their mission and seek
protection in the Presidio. When they spurned his plea, he urged them at

least to move closer to the Presidio, but again they refused. On March 15 Colonel Parrilla sent a soldier, Luis Padilla, to the mission three miles down the river with a message for Father Terreros, requesting the priests to come to the Presidio and advising them that Parrilla himself would come to the mission that afternoon to escort them. The messenger was rebuffed.[118]

In view of the circumstances, and remembering that he, Ortiz, was responsible for not only the missions' protection but also the presidio, all its inhabitants, the supply train and its escort and the soldiers guarding the animals, he afforded to the mission eight soldiers. They were all he could spare. With this contingent of soldiers, there were thirty-five residents at the mission.

In the early morning of March 16, 1758, just after Father Terreros had said Mass, screams of "Indians!" coming from the riverbank reached the mission. Those who dared to look beyond the protective outer wall were horrified to see about two thousand Indians, armed with rifles, spears and bows and arrows, dressed and bedecked for war. The Indians, seeing the front

Interior of San Sabá. *Image courtesy of author.*

gate shut and barred, saw that gaining entrance to the mission would come at some great loss to themselves. Since many of these Norteños were of the Tejas group, some were familiar to the mission's occupants. The Taovaya, who made up the majority of the attack group, used these old acquaintances to try to bribe their way into the mission. The Indians declared that they were only looking for Apaches and meant no harm to the Spanish. One of the eight soldiers at the mission, Ascensio Cadena, recognized several of the Indians as those he had helped at the San Xavier missions. To him now these same Indians stated their peaceful intentions. Cadena related to Father Terreros that he assumed the entreaties of peace were genuine.

Some accounts state that, due to the promises of nonviolence and the recognition of many of the Tejas tribes, the priests ordered the gates opened. Others relate that the Indians, after realizing the magnitude of the fear of all inside, simply dismounted, went to the gate and opened it themselves. Whatever the story, within moments the entire compound was swarming with hundreds of hostile Indians. The priests, save Father Santiesteban, who had stayed in the church kneeling at the altar, tried to pacify the Indians by handing out gifts of tobacco and other tokens. From testimony given later, a Comanche chief who accepted some of these gifts with a sneer and never dismounted his horse appeared to be in charge of the attack. It seemed the rest were following whatever this chief directed.

The Indians began crashing through the mission, grabbing whatever they could and destroying whatever they deemed to be of no value. They demanded more horses than just the few that the mission had on hand. When told there were no more, the Comanche chief asked if there were more at the presidio. The answer was "yes," and Father Terreros even volunteered to write a note to Ortiz to try to acquire them. No one can know just what Terreros's intentions really were. Most probably he had thought that he could alert the presidio of their plight and gain some sort of assistance for the others. Undoubtedly, even if he had succeeded, he knew Ortiz would not comply with such an outlandish demand. Terreros understood that this would be, in one way or another, his last effort as a missionary.

Father Terreros finished writing his note and gave it to a Tejas chief. While the chief was gone, the others continued stealing and vandalizing everything at the mission. Many of the Spanish and their charges hid in the priests' apartment. After a few minutes, the Tejas chief returned, angrily shouting that not only did Ortiz deny the request for more horses but that the soldiers had fired on them and that three of his warriors were now dead. Father Terreros, in a last effort to prevent more violence, suggested that he would ride to the presidio himself to ask for the horses. He, along with one of the soldiers, José Garcia, mounted and rode toward the main gate. As soon as the pair reached the exit, Father Terreros was shot and fell, fatally wounded. A moment later, Garcia, too, was killed instantly. The mêlée spread now that any sign of conscience or pretense was dissolved.

Knowing full well where the Spanish and the others were hiding, the Indians set fire to the area. Then, while combing room by room, other Indians came to the church where Father Santiesteban was still kneeling in prayer at the altar. He was decapitated where he knelt. His charred body was found a few days later amid the smoldering remains. His head was found later that day in a storeroom. The remains of the two martyrs were buried beside each other in the church cemetery.

After a few days of cautious and painful wandering, Father Molina, with a broken arm, and the survivors—ten in all—finally arrived at the presidio. Their escape had been made possible by a small detachment of soldiers from the presidio who, although unsuccessful in their rescue attempt, nonetheless created enough of a diversion for the others to scramble out of their hiding places and crawl toward the presidio. Two soldiers of this relief dispatch would never return, shot from their horses. A surviving soldier who made his way to San Antonio was the first to relate the horrible news. He claimed to have carried Father Molina on his back until such time that he was shot through the shoulder, assuming the bullet had first passed through the body of Molina. The later account of Molina refuted this man's story. The soldier was obviously lying, but since he was wounded and had limped all the way to San Antonio, he was never charged with an offense.

Ortiz waited four days to dare to inspect the mission ruins. (The presidio had also been attacked, but the Indians, unsure of success at the presidio, retreated sometime in the early morning hours of March 18.) Ortiz was horrified by what he witnessed. The burial of the dead took precedence over all other matters. In all, eight Spaniards died during the massacre. Even with archaeological studies carried out in the 1960s, remains of the mission have been found but no remains of the buried priests.

News of the attack spread quickly through the region, but the viceroy in Mexico did not learn of the events for twenty-three days. So informed, he ordered all available resources to the aid of San Sabá. Of course, it was all much too late.

The terror caused by so large a host of Indians spread through Nueva España much faster than did any official response. It was over a year later, in the autumn of 1759, that Colonel Parrilla Ortiz, with a force of six hundred, attempted to take revenge on the tribes of the north. The resulting chaos signaled a change in Spanish plans in the territory. As has been stated, the Native Americans, especially those of the north and east—the Comanches, Taovayas, Yanes, Tejas—armed with Spanish horses and French rifles became a force with which the meager Spanish resources simply could not compete. As a result, Santa Cruz de San Sabá Mission was never rebuilt. Strangely, maybe even ironically, Presidio San Luis de las Amarillas remained active for another fourteen years, although from 1759 on, it was generally referred to simply as Presidio de San Sabá. After the attack, the presidio was rebuilt using stone and mortar. These materials were used mainly because of the old notion that the hills contained silver, and the Spanish wanted to maintain a position there in the event more riches were found. However, the site was ordered abandoned in 1772.

The site of Mission Santa Cruz de San Sabá has never been fully recovered. The State of Texas erected a marker in 1936, but archaeological work in the 1960s discovered remnants of a Spanish settlement along the riverbank, about a mile from where the marker was placed. According to Weddle, over three hundred artifacts were recovered from this site. The site of the presidio is another matter, though.

The position of the presidio has been discovered, and a reconstructed presidio is located today just outside of Menard, Texas. However, this site, though a reconstruction based on factual, original accounting, is a reconstruction of a previous reconstruction. The original Presidio San Luis de las Amarillas would have encompassed about twice the area of the present one. During the nineteenth century, as has been mentioned, much of the stone used to build the presidio after the massacre was taken by settlers to build fences, homes and other structures. Evidently, only the main portal gate with a portion of wall was all that remained before anyone began a restoration effort in the early twentieth century. Inscriptions or graffiti by James Bowie and noted German geologist Ferdinand von Roemer, among others, were found on this portal door. In 1936–37, the Texas Centennial Commission, funded by the WPA, reconstructed the northwest portion of the presidio, that is, the front gate and tower. In 1967, surveying and field testing was undertaken by the Texas State Building Commission. Then in 1981, similar work was conducted by James Ivey of the University of Texas at San Antonio. From 2000 to 2003, the archaeology department at Texas Tech University undertook excavations and retrieved artifacts that included musket balls, nails and pottery sherds linked to the time period. The Presidio Restoration Committee and the City of Menard have now completed the presidio's reconstruction. A portion of the original acequia can still be found today in downtown Menard.

The destruction of Mission San Sabá brought about the "Red River Campaign" of Colonel Ortiz Parrilla. After submitting his report on the massacre and traveling to San Antonio, a military junta in Mexico decided that Ortiz should pursue those Norteños responsible for the attack on San Sabá. And, as stated, this action took approximately a year to materialize. One of the largest problems for Parrilla was gathering enough troops to face what was sure to be a significant Indian force and fight them in their own territory. Many of the citizens refused the summons to join ranks. As a result, Colonel Parrilla was forced to conscript a few hundred Indians and whoever else he could gather from the presidio at San Saba. The force of approximately five hundred men was a motley bunch of Lipan Apache and Tlascalan Indians, combined with regular soldiers, cowboys, carpenters and mine workers.[119] The unwillingness and fear of much of Spanish Texas and Coahuila served as advance warning to Parrilla about the expedition's outcome.

In the year between the slaughter at San Sabá Mission and Colonel Parrilla taking to the field, many Comanche raids had taken place throughout the region, resulting in many deaths. Although everyone from the viceroy to ranchers desperately wanted and needed Parrilla to be successful, no one seemed willing to make the fight his own. Colonel Parrilla was in a desperate situation; he was engaging an enemy on their own land who was greater in number and stronger in discipline.

Ortiz Parrilla located a large Taovayas settlement on the shore of the Red River. Their well-known oval-shaped huts surrounded by well-tended fields indicated to Parrilla that he had located the host enemy. That a French flag waved from the center of the complex only reinforced to the Spanish their enemy's intentions.

The Spanish were lured by a small band of mounted Indians onto the river's soft bank, where it was difficult to maneuver. Somewhat surprised that he had discovered so large a fortress, Parrilla withdrew to convene with his officers. He drew his force into fighting formation, placing the Lipans at one flank, the other Indian auxiliaries at the other flank and the Spaniards in the middle. The battle lasted four hours, during which time both flanks collapsed. Repeated advances by the Spanish were repelled by an enemy too well entrenched and supplied. The last, desperate act, as night fell, was to try and bring the cannons to effect. Only two were able to be positioned, and these, as Weddle writes, "were fired eleven times at the fort, but the Indians only mocked the effect."[120] The Spanish withdrew, and the cannons were left behind. During that evening's conference, Colonel Parrilla learned that many of his Indian allies had fled. From the starting total of five hundred, only fifty-two were now either dead, wounded or missing. The officers were all for returning to San Sabá. A demoralized Parrilla had to agree, and the Spanish began a steady withdrawal.

The Red River Campaign was not so much a military loss, but it did ensure that Colonel Parrilla would be replaced as commander of the largest and most important presidio in the province. His replacement, though, would shock many.

For eight years, Captain Felipe Rábago y Terán had been sitting in a cell in Mexico, trying to explain if and why he had ordered the murder of a fellow soldier and a Franciscan priest. Even though the Indian Andrés had at first confessed to killing the priest on Rábago's orders, he had quickly recanted his story. For whatever reason, this was good enough for the Mexican officials. After again claiming that the murders at San Xavier had been committed by the Coco Indians (who were conveniently absent and unable to speak for themselves), Rábago and Andrés were acquitted by the interim viceroy, Coaxial de la Vega. Rábago's reinstatement into the military and subsequent command of Presidio de San Luis de Amarillas has been described as remarkable; quite an understatement, given his history. Colonel Parrilla even decried the appointment and described Rábago as a young man with more money than judgment. Another of Rábago's detractors was Father Mariano de Dolores, who had witnessed firsthand the nefarious machinations of this captain. However, it appears that, while incarcerated, Rábago had gained the friendship of Father Diego Jiménez, who had been, years before, one of the original six Franciscans assigned to Mission San Sabá. Armed with Father Jiménez's recommendation and the recantation of Andrés, de la Vega ordered that Rábago be reinstated as commander of Presidio San Francisco Xavier de Gigedo. However, since that presidio did not exist any longer and its soldiers had been garrisoned at San Luis de las Amarillas, it was decided that Rábago should be given that assignment. A meeting between Parrilla and the new commander was scheduled, and the two officers met at Parrilla's home in the summer of 1760. Ortiz Parrilla asked Rábago to please look after the several personal items Parrilla had left at the presidio. Rábago agreed, but he was clearly only interested in slandering the good name of the garrison's former commander by making the Red River Campaign appear to have been some enormously humiliating Spanish defeat when, in reality, it was more of a victory than most realized. As Robert Weddle wrote:

> *And so the seasoned military commander, accustomed as he was to having his orders obeyed when ordering his men into battle, succumbed to the blandishments of an inveterate con man. As for Rábago, he soon would be on the frontier, out of the viceroy's reach, as well as Ortiz Parrilla's.*[121]

The presidio's new commanding officer arrived at San Sabá in late September 1760, having journeyed around San Antonio because of the harsh feelings many of the religious still held for him there.

Some have written that Captain Rábago had, indeed, had a change of heart while in jail. These same commentators have written that it is entirely possible that, having confessed to Jiménez of his crimes, he truly was ready and prepared to undertake service for the crown again. Even Father Morfi, not one easily swayed by sentiment, suggested that perhaps Rábago's change of heart was an attempt to make amends to religion by accepting this new and most important assignment. And the assignment was supposed to have been extremely important.

One of the commander's orders was to try to open a more northern trade route between Texas and New Mexico. Given the strength, numbers and skill of the Comanche and Taovayas tribes who lived in the area, this task would be difficult for anyone. Rábago did send out an exploratory group of forty soldiers to reconnoiter to the west. The troops advanced as far as the Pecos River and returned almost one month after setting out. This expedition did chart out the areas visited, mapping water supplies and the topography. All of this would have been valuable information for further expeditions—expeditions that Rábago would not busy himself with. The new commander was about to prove that he really could not be trusted so much after all.

Felipe Rábago y Terán was very interested in new construction. Within one year of his assignment, he had almost completed the total reconstruction of the presidio at San Sabá, replacing the logs with stone-and-mortar fortifications and digging a moat around the grounds until the presidio resembled a castle. The garrison even took on a new name, Real Presidio de San Sabá. But Rábago was not finished establishing new buildings.

Rábago, eager to renew the efforts begun with the San Sabá mission by strengthening the Spanish relationship with the Lipan Apaches, began to invite the Apache chiefs for interviews at the presidio, where he promised to construct new missions for them. The trouble lay not in the building of these new missions but in the fact that the viceroy wanted them built northwest of San Sabá. Rábago allowed the Apache to decide where they wanted their new missions, and they chose sites almost exactly in the opposite direction.

Without consulting his government, Captain Rábago began construction along the Nueces River of Mission San Lorenzo de la Santa Cruz in January 1762. The site was almost equidistant between San Juan Bautista and San Antonio. For the missionaries' supplies, Rábago asked his friend Father Jiménez, since he was not at liberty to request help from the authorities in Mexico. Father Jiménez came to serve at this new mission. He was accompanied by Father Joaquín de Baños, who had been assigned to Mission San Sabá years before.

Having placed a small contingent of soldiers at Mission San Lorenzo, Rábago planned to return to his presidio. Just before leaving, another Apache chief, El Turnio, asked for another mission for his people. Rábago, flattered, agreed. One month later, Mission Nuestra Señora de la Candelabra del Cañon was constructed; again Father Jiménez took charge of the spiritual needs of this community. For a moment things seemed to be going Rábago's way. As Weddle points out, "It was customary in founding new missions to obtain approval of the mother college—in this case the College of Querétaro—and the viceroy. Father Jiménez had taken care of the first step. The second was not so easy."[122]

Of course, the viceroy's office learned of the missions. Both Father Jiménez and Captain Rábago declared the need for the missions. In fact, so great was the need that the captain now asked that his presidio be moved to the area, because, he claimed, the constant shifting of his troops between San Sabá and the Valle de San José (where the two new missions were located) lessened the security and effectiveness of both. This time, though, as with all of us, fate would decide the issue.

At the end of the Seven Years' War, France delivered Louisiana to Spain, thereby ending the threat of French encroachment into Texas. The Spanish government, ever mindful of its expenses, no longer saw reason to fortify the region against a vanished French presence. As things stood, the crown was having difficulty appropriating funds to defend a frontier that was now theirs. In March 1763, the fiscal auditor, Don Domingo Valcárcel, stated that he saw little hope for the two new missions. In fact, he also believed that the presidio at San Sabá was now useless.

During the next few years, conditions at the missions of El Cañon and the San Sabá Presidio deteriorated. At the missions, the Apache Indians would leave to hunt or attack their enemies or simply plunder the countryside. Oftentimes, their pursuits led them into Coahuila, where they conducted raids. As such, Rábago received complaints that his two missions had been placed too close to the border. Furthermore, maintenance of the missions was wearing on the captain. Without government support, Rábago was forced to allow the Apaches to hunt outside the mission for their food, often not returning. Next, the Comanches, tiring of the constant Apache raids, began to drive farther into central Texas to get their revenge. And the presidio was now under steady attack and losing its viability as a defensive installment; the northern tribes were wearing it down. Again, the number of attacks, killings and thefts is beyond the range of this book. Suffice to say that these crimes increased in number and severity as the years passed.

In 1767, the king's inspector visited Texas. As has already been mentioned, the Marqués de Rubí made several sweeping reforms to all of Spain's claims in the New World. And, as mentioned before, Rubí saw benefit for presidios only along the southern portion of Spain's dominion and thought that only Santa Fe and San Antonio should warrant any further regal support. As for Captain Rábago, this report, coupled with the other distresses, signaled

the end. The presidio was abandoned in 1772, and the missions of El Cañon suffered the same fate. By 1767, there were no more Franciscans trying to convert the Lipans at Mission de la Candelaria; those who had been stationed at San Lorenzo were transferred to Arizona in 1771.

As is evident from history, the relationship between the Spanish and the Apache Nation also deteriorated after this time. The aggression by both sides was intense and prolonged. For the Franciscans, in the end politics and the determined arm of the military drove them away. Secularization ensured that

Portrait of St. Francis, Mission Concepción. *Image courtesy of author.*

each mission either disappeared from the landscape or was left to waste away until some other hand took notice and sympathy. Few of us could ever hope to have the determination and charity that these men showed for others who, at times, were hostile, dangerous or unwilling. That several of these missions are, today, still active churches is a great testament to the zeal, aspirations and faith possessed by these men.

Conclusion

The settlement of Nueva España and, for the purposes of this book, Texas ultimately begins, of course, with Christopher Columbus. However, closer to home, as it were, the event that actually began expansion into the Texas region was the Cortés invasion of Mexico. The sheer amount of wealth that Cortés laid upon the Spanish crown's table was so immense that every statesman, explorer and adventurer took notice and wanted to participate. Many did come from around the world, each imagining that the New World would somehow be better than the one they were leaving behind. Of course, not all who arrived in America in its early years came by choice. The hundreds of thousands of Spanish, French and English soldiers who were conscripted to serve often came unwillingly to serve a government whose machinations meant very little to them. However, there was one group who came voluntarily to serve and who, simultaneously, understood the difficulties that lay ahead.

It is difficult, from our modern vantage point, to understand just how harsh the frontier reaching from Louisiana to California must have been for the Franciscans, Dominicans and Jesuits. The Franciscans, at least, according to their order, very often walked from their colleges in México across the Rio Grande and into whichever region of Texas they were assigned or chose. It is hoped that the small amount of information offered here will allow the reader some capacity to understand what an incredible thing it was for these priests to stride into sometimes violent, always unfamiliar land and proudly step forward to make contact to begin a relationship, not of subjugation but of salvation, for that is how they viewed the issue.

The reader might also realize that, while the Franciscans are the main focus of this book, the narrative often strayed to the Spanish government and those soldiers and officials involved with the government's work. This is unavoidable, as often the Franciscans could not progress without financial support from the government offices in Mexico or Madrid and the consequent military assistance. The crown held the purse strings and was very reluctant to open wide that pouch unless it was receiving funds in exchange for doling them out. In fact, several historians have blamed this miserliness of the Spanish government for the early and ultimate loss of Mexico and Texas as colonies. Coupled with this pecuniary reluctance, it is also believed that the slowness of the dispatches between the missions and Mexico, and Mexico with Madrid or Seville, typically taking months in each case, was the other factor in Spain's loss of control. As stated in this book, the missionaries were often left alone, ill supplied and ill protected. Requests for help passed over hundreds of hard miles, only to be placed on some official's desk in Mexico, where the decisions took longer to play out than did the situations that warranted their attention.

Also, readers with a knowledge of this subject will undoubtedly ask themselves why this book does not cover every Spanish mission and presidio that at one time or another was placed somewhere in the Texas region. The simple answer is that the parameters of this book were set short; there was not a great deal of room to account for each construction attempt. Likewise, many of the Spanish missions are simply no longer standing. The missions of east Texas, for example, are all gone, having been allowed to slip back into the woods from where they came. These are not enumerated here within their own chapter, simply because most of them are referred to as the progenitors of other missions. Others along the Rio Grande were victims of the river's swelling. Still others, like Mission Nuestra Señora del Refugio (Texas's last mission, from 1793), are mere shells. Today, Our Lady of Refuge Catholic Church stands directly on the site of the old mission. Sources state that some of the original construction can still be seen under the present building.[123] Likewise, the Rancho de las Cabras (Ranch of the Goats), the cattle ranch supplying Mission San Francisco de la Espada—sometimes listed as Mission de las Cabras because there was a chapel on site—is a semi-active archaeological site, one that has been excavated but has been covered over to protect whatever might remain. And San Fernando Cathedral in downtown San Antonio was a very active mission and religious center for the Villa de

Portrait of the Virgin of Guadalupe at San Fernando Cathedral. *Image courtesy of author.*

Béxar. Any one of these missions or presidios could be the subject of a book itself (and many are), but to explore every one of the stories here would have been impossible.[124]

Reference should also be made to the amazing number of discrepancies among sources as to dates, places and other information. Since most of the missions were transient, and each location attracted hundreds if not thousands of individuals, it is likely that different authors would present different calculations or theories. In this book, the author has tried to triangulate the information after gathering as many sources as possible and drawing conclusions after much research. Undoubtedly others will be able to locate sources that disagree with some of the numbers, dates or locations given here. However, it should be understood that the Franciscans and Spanish authorities were, while slow to act at times, nevertheless very accurate record-keepers. The number of available inventory lists, baptismal and marriage records and other documents is exact and plentiful. It should be noted that many writers have not made use of these materials as much as they might have.

Lastly, the missions, the presidios and the Franciscans' work would never have occurred if not for the Native Americans who inhabited the land before the Spanish or French arrived. This author, while a native Texan, was amazed at the dozens and dozens of Indian group names appearing within the state of Texas alone. Also interesting is the fact that many of these names have survived to us in their Spanish form rather than in their native language. This is due to an ethnocentrism not lost on many historians and writers. The name of one tribe, for example, the Manos de Perro (Dog Hands), appears very often in the Franciscans' records from Mission Valero. Vincent Huízar, in the course of his research on the missions in the San Antonio area alone, has listed approximately seventy different tribes that gathered, at one time or another, at these missions. While it is true that several of these tribes might belong to a larger confederacy or group, each was distinctive in its dialect, mode of living, dress and behavior. The regional politics and infighting that existed among these tribes has been discussed here, and its effect on the Franciscans' missionary work cannot be overstated. The Franciscans tried to mollify some of these age-old hostilities by encouraging intermarriage among different tribes and having natives live, worship and work side by side, to create something that had not existed before. The final appeal to gather the Apaches into missions was, at its core, an effort to quell the violence among these many Native American groups. However, as has been seen, settling into confined areas was not an idea that came easily to many of these peoples. While some, like the Jumanos, actively sought out the religious and conversion, others, like the Lipan Apaches, exasperated the friars by using the missions' assets only for their own ends. Still, taken in its entirety, the story of the Franciscans' attempts to bring to these people what they believed was the ultimate good is one of the most fantastic stories this country has recorded.[125]

NOTES

Chapter 1

1. Bernal Diaz de Castillo, *The Memoirs of the Conquistador Bernal Diaz del Castillo, Written by Himself Containing a True and Full Account of the Discovery and Conquest of Mexico and New Spain*, trans. John Ingram Lockhart, vol. 1 (London, 1844; repr., Project Gutenberg, 2010), 374, www.gutenberg.org/files/32474-h.htm.
2. Robert S. Weddle, *The San Saba Mission* (College Station: Texas A&M University Press, 1999), 28.
3. Herbert Eugene Bolton, *Spanish Exploration in the Southwest, 1542–1706* (New York: Charles Scribner's Sons, 1916), 284. Digitized copy, Americana Collection, Harvard University, https://archive.org/stream/spanishexplorat0-3boltgoog_djvu.txt.
4. Robert S. Weddle, *San Juan Bautista, Gateway to Spanish Texas* (Austin: University of Texas Press, 1991), 6.
5. Henri Joutel, "Joutel's Journal of La Salle's Last Voyage 1684–7. With a Frontispiece of Gudebrod's Statue of La Salle and the Map of the Original French Edition, Paris 1713, in Facsimile" (Albany, NY: Joseph McDonough, 1906), 61. Internet Archive, http://archive.org/details/joutelsjournalof00joutrich.
6. Ibid., 83.
7. Ibid., 134.
8. Weddle, *San Juan Bautista*, 10.
9. Father Damián Massanet, "Letter of Fray Damián Massanet to Don Carlos de Sigüenza 1690." American Journeys Collection. Document

No. AJ-018, 354–55. Wisconsin Historical Society Digital Library and Archives. Wisconsin Historical Society, 2003. www.americanjourneys. org/pdf/AJ-018.pdf.

10. Alonso de León, "Itinerary of the Expedition Made by General Alonzo DeLeon for the Discovery of the Bahia del Espíritu Santo and the French Settlement. 168," *Quarterly of the Texas State Historical Association* 8, no. 3 (January 1905): 216–17. www.jstor.org/stable/30242792.

11. Walter F. McCaleb, *Spanish Missions of Texas* (San Antonio, TX: Naylor, 1961), 32.

12. Ibid., 37.

13. R.C. Clark, "The Beginnings of Texas: Fort Saint Louis and Mission San Francisco de los Tejas," *Quarterly of the Texas State Historical Association* 5, no. 3 (January 1902): 197–98. https://books.google.com/books.

Chapter 2

14. John L. Kessell, *Spain in the Southwest: A Narrative History of Colonial New Mexico, Arizona, Texas, and California* (Norman: University of Oklahoma Press, 2002), 167–68.

15. Weddle, *San Juan Bautista*, 100.

16. Eleanor Claire Buckley, "The Aguayo Expedition into Texas and Louisiana, 1719–1722," *Quarterly of the Texas State Historical Association* 15, no. 1 (July 1911): 2. www.jstor.org/stable/30243078.

17. Fray Isidro Félix de Espinosa, *Crónica de los Colegios de Propaganda Fide de la Nueva España*. New edition with notes and introduction by Lino G. Canedo, OFM (Washington, D.C., 1964), 737. https://archive.org/ stream/cronicadeloscole00espi#page/n11/mode/2up.

18. Ibid., 738.

19. Buckley, "Aguayo Expedition," 13.

20. Ibid., 22.

21. Ibid., 60.

22. Weddle, *San Juan Bautista*, 167.

23. Ibid., 222.

24. "Father Gaspar José de Solis: The Expedition of Father Gaspar Jose de Solis into Texas, 1767–1768" (master's thesis submitted and translated by George Howden, University of California, Berkeley, 1915), 45–55. http://hdl.handle.net/2027/uc1.

25. McCaleb, *Spanish Missions of Texas*, 88.

26. Jacinto Quirarte, *The Art and Architecture of the Texas Missions* (Austin: University of Texas Press, 2002), 25.

Chapter 3

27. James Brook, "Oñate's Missing Foot." http://pages.ucsd.edu/~rfrank/class_web/ES-112A/Onate.html.

28. Fray Alonso de Benavides, "The Memorial of Fray Alonso de Benavides 1630," trans. Mrs. Edwards E. Ayer (Chicago, 1916; repr., Albuquerque, NM: privately published, 1965), 13. http://hdl.handle.net/2027/mdp.

29. Ibid., 18.

30. Ibid.

31. Ibid., 35.

32. Ibid., 58–59.

33. Anne E. Hughes, "The Beginnings of Spanish Settlement in the El Paso District," *University of California Publications in History* 1 (Berkeley: University of California, 1914): 311–12. https://archive.org/stream/beginningsofspani00hughrich#page/312/mode/2up.

34. Charles Wilson Hackett, ed., "Revolt of the Pueblo Indians of New Mexico and Otermin's Attempted Reconquest, 1680–1682" (Albuquerque: University of New Mexico Press, 1942), vol. 9, 248. Wisconsin Historical Society, 2003. http://www.americanjourneys.org/aj-009b.

35. Ibid., 245.

36. James Wakefield Burke, *Missions of Old Texas* (Cranbury, NJ: A.S. Barnes and Co., 1971), 115.

37. Rex E. Gerald, "Archaeological Studies Related to the Reroofing of the Socorro Church. January–March 1984." Rex E. Gerald Papers, Special Archives, University of Texas at El Paso, Box 4.

38. *El Paso Times,* "Help! Socorro Mission Cries for Aid," October 22, 1978.

39. Rex E. Gerald, "Report on Archaeological Monitoring of Light Pole Installation Activities at the Socorro Mission National Register Site. May 27, 1986." Rex E. Gerald Papers, Special Archives of University of Texas at El Paso, Box 4.

40. Magda Madureira Trujillo, interview with author, March 2016.

41. Hughes, "Beginnings of Spanish Settlement," 392.

Chapter 4

42. Marion A. Habig, OFM, *The Alamo Chain of Missions: A History of San Antonio's Five Old Missions* (Chicago: Franciscan Herald Press, 1968; repr., Pioneer Enterprises, 1997), 40.

43. Ibid., 40–41.

44. Burke, *Missions of Old Texas*, 122.

45. Adina de Zavala, *History and Legends of the Alamo and Other Missions in and around San Antonio* (San Antonio, TX: self-published, 1917), 10. http://archive.org/details/historylegendsof00zava.

46. Quirarte, *Art and Architecture of the Texas Missions*, 55.

47. Burke, *Missions of Old Texas*, 142.

48. Quirarte, *Art and Architecture of the Texas Missions*, 51–52.

49. Susan Prendergast Schoelwer, "San Antonio de Valero Mission," Handbook of Texas Online. Accessed June 10, 2016. http://www.tshaonline.org/handbook/online/articles/uqs08.

50. Fray Isidro Félix de Espinosa, *Crónica de los Colegios de Propaganda Fide de la Nueva España* (Washington, D.C., 1964), 812. https://archive.org/stream/cronicadeloscole00espi#page/n11/mode/2up.

51. Quirarte, *Art and Architecture of the Texas Missions*, 70.

52. Burke, *Missions of Old Texas*, 96.

53. Mary A. Maverick, *Memoirs of Mary A. Maverick* (San Antonio, TX: Alamo Printing Co., 1921), 22. https://archive.org/stream/memoirsmarymav00mavegoog#page/n8/mode/2up.

54. Biofile of Building Artisans Who Worked on the Northern Spanish Borderlands of New Spain and Early Mexico, comp. Mardith Schuetz-Miller for National Park Service (Tucson, AZ: n.d.).

55. Vincent Huízar, interview with author, June 2016.

56. Fray Juan Augustin Morfi, "History of Texas 1673–1779" (San Antonio, TX: National Park Service, 1935), 3–4. "Historic American Buildings Survey, Addendum to: Mission San José y San Miguel de Aguayo."

57. Habig, *Alamo Chain of Missions*, 99.

58. Ibid., 102.

59. Ibid., 111.

60. John Russell Bartlett, *Personal Narrative of Explorations and Incidents in Texas, New Mexico, California, Sonora and Chihuahua* (New York: D. Appleton Co., 1856), 43.

61. Habig, *Alamo Chain of Missions*, 113.

62. Ibid., 114.

63. Quirarte, *Art and Architecture of the Texas Missions*, 97.

64. Burke, *Missions of Old Texas*, 107.

65. Quirarte, *Art and Architecture of the Texas Missions*, 105.

66. Habig, *Alamo Chain of Missions*, 129.

67. Ibid., 135

68. Ibid., 141.

69. Ibid., 147.

70. Burke, *Missions of Old Texas*, 109.

71. Bartlett, *Personal Narrative of Explorations*, 44–45.

72. Father David Garcia (administrator Mission Concepción), interview with author, June 2016.

73. Rebecca Roberts, "Restoring San Antonio's Spanish Missions," *Texas Society of Architects* (May/June 2013). https://texasarchitects.org/v/article-detail/Restoring-San-Antonio-s-Spanish-Misions/dq/.

74. Habig, *Alamo Chain of Missions*, 160.

75. Quirarte, *Art and Architecture of the Texas Missions*, 131.

76. Burke, *Missions of Old Texas*, 89.

77. Weddle, *San Juan Bautista*, 211.

78. Ibid.

79. Habig, *Alamo Chain of Missions*, 163.

80. Weddle, *San Juan Bautista*, 213–14.

81. Habig, *Alamo Chain of Missions*, 167.

82. Ibid., 180.

83. Quirarte, *Art and Architecture of the Texas Missions*, 141.

84. Burke, *Missions of Old Texas*, 90.

85. James T. Escobedo Jr., "Bouchu, Francis," Handbook of Texas Online, accessed June 13, 2016. http://tshaonline.org/handbook/online/articles/fbo84.

86. Habig, *Alamo Chain of Missions*, 187.

87. Father David Garcia in conversation with author, June 2016.

88. Garcia, interview with author, June 2016.

89. De Espinosa, *Crónica de los Colegios*, 679.

90. Habig, *Alamo Chain of Missions*, 201.

91. Burke, *Missions of Old Texas*, 85.

92. Habig, *Alamo Chain of Missions*, 202.

93. Ibid., 204–05.

94. Ibid., 205.

95. Quirarte, *Art and Architecture of the Texas Missions*, 149.

96. Habig, *Alamo Chain of Missions*, 213.

97. Ibid., 215.

98. Ibid., 224.

99. Ibid., 226.

100. Quirarte, *Art and Architecture of the Texas Missions*, 157.

101. Garcia, interview with author, June 2016.

Chapter 5

102. Loan E. Supplee, "San Xavier Missions," Handbook of Texas Online, accessed July 14, 2016. http://www/tshaonline.org.handbook/online/articles/uqs34.

103. Herbert E. Bolton, "The Founding of the Missions on the San Gabriel River, 1745–1749," *Southwestern Historical Quarterly* 17, no. 4 (1914): 323–78. http://www.jstor.org/stable/30234610.

104. Robert S. Weddle, *After the Massacre: The Violent Legacy of the San Sabá Mission* (Lubbock: Texas Tech University Press, 2007), 30–31.

105. Weddle, *San Saba Mission*, 33.

106. Ibid., 34.

107. As so often happens with other sources, here McCaleb mistakenly refers to the Apache as the aggressors that morning and infers that Ceballos was one of the religious. There were only two Lipan Apaches in the compound, and they, with Father Molina, escaped.

108. McCaleb, *Spanish Missions of Texas*, 75.

109. Weddle, *San Saba Mission*, 35.

110. William Edward Dunn, "The Apache Mission on the San Saba River: Its Founding and Failure," *Southwestern Historical Quarterly* 17, no. 4 (1914): 379–414. http://www.jstor.org/stable/30234611.

111. Weddle, *San Saba Mission*, 36–37.

112. Dunn, "Apache Mission on the San Saba River," 394.

113. Weddle, *San Saba Mission*, 54.

114. Hubert Howe Bancroft, "The Works of Hubert Howe Bancroft; Volume XV. History of the North Mexican States vol. I 1531–1800" (San Francisco: A.L. Bancroft & Company, 1884), 645–46.

115. Weddle, *San Saba Mission*, 59.

116. Dunn, "Apache Mission on the San Saba River," 401.

117. Ibid., 402. This is an approximation by Dunn, however, probably an accurate one.

118. Weddle, *San Saba Mission*, 69.

119. Henry Easton Allen, "The Parrilla Expedition to the Red River in 1759," *Southwestern Historical Quarterly* 43, no. 1 (1939): 53–71. http://www.jstor.org/stable/30235858.
120. Weddle, *San Saba Mission*, 121.
121. Weddle, *After the Massacre*, 41. Weddle makes frequent reference to the fact that, for Parrilla and the Spanish, the Red River Campaign was, generally, a success. It was, according to Weddle, Rábago who kept insisting it had not been.
122. Weddle, *San Saba Mission*, 158.

Conclusion

123. June Melby Benowitz, "Nuestra Senora Del Refugio Mission," Handbook of Texas Online, accessed July 6, 2016. http://www.tshaonline.org/handbook/online/articles/uqn18.
124. Burke's *Missions of Old Texas* contains an excellent map and lists of all the missions and presidios in the state.
125. Habig's *Alamo Chain of Missions* contains an excellent appendix of the many Franciscans who worked at the missions within Texas.

INDEX

About the Author

Byron Browne is a writer and teacher living in Austin, Texas, with his wife, Angie. He has written on subjects as varied as bullfights in Spain and the viticulture industry in west Texas.